Seánín Hoy, Gearóid O'Brien and Stephen O'Brien have crafted and curated a pedagogically-rich repository of frameworks, activities and worksheets to support post-primary teachers in their global citizenship education teaching. This vital resource addresses some of the most defining and pressing global issues of our time – ranging from migration, displacement and belonging, to disinformation. Each activity is scaffolded by a rich conceptual framework that promotes critical habits of mind, such as metacognitive thinking, epistemic humility and imagination. This resource is sure to guarantee high levels of student engagement and to promote deep and ethically-responsive understandings of core global citizenship education themes, values and principles.

Dr. Audrey Bryan, Associate Professor of Sociology, School of Human Development, Dublin City University

This book is a welcome addition to the resources available to teachers in Ireland working in the exciting – and challenging – field of global citizenship. In this fast-changing area, it is important that teachers have tried and tested materials suitable for use in the classroom. This sensitively-written text gives learners the information and the methods needed to address current issues in a searching and balanced way. The chapters are well-chosen and clearly laid out, with detailed background information and numerous exercises that can easily be put into action. Across areas from 'identity' to 'migration', from 'stereotypes' to 'moral dilemmas', this book provides a rich resource for teachers looking to plan lessons and keep their learners engaged with vital global issues.

Dr. Edward Lahiff, Senior Lecturer in International Development, University College Cork

A Teacher's Handbook on Global Citizenship Education in the Post-primary Classroom is an invaluable resource for educators aiming to foster global awareness and critical thinking in their students. With 10 thoughtfully-crafted lessons, this *Handbook* addresses complex, crucial topics, such as: Identity; stereotypes; moral dilemmas; migration; seeking asylum; and media literacy. Written by teachers for teachers, it provides practical, adaptable strategies that build upon foundational GCE concepts. For any practitioner committed to incorporating GCE and social justice topics into their learning environment, this resource offers essential guidance and a flexible framework to nurture informed, compassionate global citizens. A must-have for every post-primary classroom.

Dr. Joanne O'Flaherty, Associate Professor & Ubuntu Research Lead, University of Limerick

A Teacher's Handbook on
GLOBAL CITIZENSHIP EDUCATION
in the Post-primary Classroom

Seánín Hoy, Gearóid O'Brien
& Stephen O'Brien

Published by OAK TREE PRESS, Cork T12 XY2N, Ireland
www.oaktreepress.com / www.SuccessStore.com

© 2024 Seánín Hoy, Gearóid O'Brien & Stephen O'Brien

A catalogue record of this book is available from the British Library.

ISBN 978 1 78119 640-3 (paperback)
ISBN 978 1 78119 641-0 (PDF)
ISBN 978 1 78119 642-7 (ePub)
ISBN 978 1 78119 643-4 (Kindle)

Cover design: Kieran O'Connor Design
Front cover illustration: Laoise Corcoran, Ursuline College, Blackrock, Cork
Back cover illustrations: Lucy McCarthy, Leila Crilly, Sally-Anne Flaherty & Auden Boyle, Ursuline College, Blackrock, Cork
Images in text: As acknowledged / 123rf.com / Shutterstock.com

All rights reserved. No part of this publication may be reproduced or transmitted in any form or by any means, including photocopying and recording, without written permission of the publisher. Such written permission must also be obtained before any part of this publication is stored in a retrieval system of any nature. Requests for permission should be directed to Oak Tree Press at info@oaktreepress.com.

CONTENTS

Acknowledgements	vi
Introduction	viii
Lesson 1: Global Citizenship Education	**1**
Lesson 2: Exploring Our Own Identity	**14**
Lesson 3: I am From…	**21**
Lesson 4: Home Is Where Our Hearts Are	**28**
Lesson 5: Our Multiple Identities	**38**
Lesson 6: Exploring Stereotypes	**51**
Lesson 7: Moral Dilemmas	**59**
Lesson 8: Migration	**70**
Lesson 9: Seeking Asylum	**88**
Lesson 10: Media	**107**
Developing as a Global Citizenship Educator through Reflective Practice	122
References	145
About the Authors	150

ACKNOWLEDGEMENTS

The authors would like to gratefully acknowledge the support of the Ubuntu Network in producing this *Handbook*. The Ubuntu Network is a community of educators in post-primary Initial Teacher Education, funded by Irish Aid, that work to support Global Citizenship Education (GCE) across Ireland. We are grateful for the ongoing support of Deirdre Hogan, National Co-Ordinator, and all the Network's partners who continue to provide excellent support for student teachers in doing GCE work. We extend our appreciation too to those Non-Governmental Organisations (NGOs) who significantly scaffold GCE supports for teacher educators – special mention here goes to Vicky Donnelly of Galway One World Centre and Financial Justice Ireland. We wish to acknowledge the steadfast support of our colleague, Sinéad O'Donovan, Administrative Officer in the School of Education, University College Cork, for her professional financial guidance over the years. We are grateful to our academic and GCE activist colleagues – Associate Professor Audrey Bryan of Dublin City University; Dr Edward Lahiff, Senior Lecturer in International Development, University College Cork; and Dr Joanne O'Flaherty, Associate Professor and Ubuntu Research Lead, University of Limerick – for their critical reviews of our work and for their considered testimonials. A sincere thank you to Brian O'Kane, Founder/Publisher at Oak Tree Press for his constant guidance and expert editorial assistance and to Kieran O'Connor for his creative work on the book cover design. We are very grateful to Dr Brian Murphy and Dr Niamh Dennehy, Director and Deputy Director of the Professional Master of Education (PME) programme in University College Cork, for their enduring collaboration and drive to further integrate GCE into Initial Teacher Education provision. We are indebted to our families, friends and work colleagues for their constant encouragement and support. And, finally, we are indebted to all the participants who directly contributed to this *Handbook* – especially the students in Ursuline College, Blackrock and Christian Brothers College in Cork and to the student teachers on the Professional Master of Education (PME) programme in University College Cork (UCC). To these participants, we extend our deepest appreciation. Your collective efforts have significantly shaped this *Handbook*.

This resource is funded by Irish Aid at the Department of Foreign Affairs (DFA) via the Ubuntu Network. Irish Aid is the Government's overseas development programme, which supports partners working in some of the world's poorest countries. Irish Aid also supports Global Citizenship Education in Ireland to encourage learning and public engagement with global issues. The ideas, opinions and comments herein are entirely the responsibility of its authors and do not necessarily represent or reflect DFA, Ubuntu and/or UCC policy.

INTRODUCTION

This *Handbook* is written *by* teachers *for* teachers. It seeks to support those new to the profession, as well as those who are already experienced in post-primary school and further education settings. Our *Teacher's Handbook* is designed to sustain these professionals in their important – relational and pedagogical – work with children and young adults. It comprises 10 scaffolded lessons, the first of which is centred on exploring the foundational discipline of Global Citizenship Education (GCE). Each subsequent lesson focuses on a global theme and on creative ways to critically engage students in their own learning about the world. While the list is not exhaustive, the global themes include:

- Our own identity;
- Belonging;
- Inter-relationships;
- Stereotypes;
- Migration;
- Seeking asylum;
- The role of the media.

Each lesson follows the same structure:

- Its particular purpose;
- Guidance for the teacher;
- The teacher materials used;
- Activities and prompts;
- Final lesson reflections;
- Additional lesson resources, which are fully referenced at the end of this *Handbook*.

This *Handbook* is particularly, though not exclusively, suited to the Transition Year (TY) programme in Irish post-primary schools. It may even inspire new short courses at this level. More broadly, this *Handbook* serves as both a conceptual and practical toolkit for how we might think and act differently in our learning responses to a changed and changing world. Education has an inherent power to transform fixed forms of knowledge, skills, attitudes and values, and to positively impact citizenry. GCE holds a special 'anchoring' power in our navigation of 'disruptive' change, including how we cope with climate destruction, civic injustice, protracted wars, rising social inequality, identity prejudice and forced migration (O'Brien, 2024). GCE teachers, in particular, play a critical role in meeting these challenges, cultivating hope and re-imagining a better world.

GCE in the Classroom

This *Handbook* is dedicated to teachers who do GCE work in the classroom. By engaging with this values-based epistemology, we argue that educators can begin to think more, and become better informed, about their everyday encounters in the world. For students and teachers, GCE presents as a critical opportunity to examine one's ('implicated') positionings with Others and our shared planet (Rothberg, 2019; Bryan, 2022). For educators, in particular, GCE can help them steer their own personal/professional journeys; even to the point where they can positively redirect their core educational identity, knowledge and values.

Whilst GCE is a distinct field of study, it has emerged from a mesh of inter-related disciplines, including critical feminism, postcolonial theory, social class theory, critical race theory, disability studies, queer theory, interculturalism and critical postmodernism. GCE is ultimately focused on developing a world informed by the core values of social justice, equality and sustainability. Its pedagogical intent, therefore, is to employ education as an effective (and affective) means of nurturing active citizenry. In essence, the education element of GCE is concerned with teaching and learning through a global justice lens. In this way, GCE draws on a range of pedagogical traditions, including *inter alia*:

- Development Education (DE);
- Human Rights Education;
- Education for Sustainable Development (ESD);
- Environmental Education;
- Multicultural Education;
- Indigenous Education; and
- Critical Pedagogy or 'Praxis'.

Mutually, such perspectives emphasise the key role of the educator in enabling, *via* democratic, creative and active-based methods, all learners to cultivate their global citizenry knowledge, skills, values and attitudes. This means enhancing learners' awareness, understandings, principles, feelings and 'know-how' in relation to (or alongside) an ever-changing, interdependent and unequal world (Irish Aid, 2017). It means finding an epistemological base – GCE is a 'joint fit' here – to critically examine the root causes of global-local justice issues and explore our own responsible actions in the world. Especially in times of 'disruptive' change, it means offering educators inspiration and hope to make some positive difference (however small).

Doing GCE work is itself inter-dependent on conditions of possibility and/or constraint both within education systems and without. Within the system, there are inspiring educator role models who remain dedicated to 'responsive' or 'sustainable' teaching (Ladson-Billings, 1995). This is particularly true of GCE champions in schools: those with a strong vocational commitment, those who care-fully reflect on their important democratic role and those who nurture, with students and peers, informed critical literacy and social action advances. At the same time, it is often a struggle – even for those committed teachers – to authentically engage with GCE work inside the education system. This is especially the case in environments where 'product' approaches to pedagogy and performative measures of 'success' are deeply embedded (O'Brien, 2016). Consequently, the cultural capacity for meaningful GCE effort is restricted and it is left to committed individuals to perform – often against the odds – its most valuable work (Bryan, 2011). With respect to influences from outside (that are nonetheless related to) the education system, Daly *et al.* (2016) especially critique 'trickle down' economic growth (read as, the endless neoliberal 'development' model) that often reproduces (not redresses) global-local forms of inequality. The point to be made here is that 'development' remains as much an incomplete project in the Global North, as it is in the Global South. There are, however, some signs of progression – at least 'officially'. At supra-national state level, for example, there is increasing validation for GCE since it promotes a "sense of belonging to a broader community" and serves as a way of "understanding, acting and relating oneself to others and the environment in space and in time…" (UNESCO, 2014, p.14). At a national level, the (second) National Strategy on Education for Sustainable Development in Ireland, entitled *ESD to 2030* (Government of Ireland, 2022), provides a framework to support and steer the contribution of the education sector around five key action areas:

- Advancing policy;
- Transforming learning environments;
- Building capacities of educators;
- Empowering and mobilising young people;
- Accelerating local level actions.

With a focus on teachers' professional development, it is noteworthy that the new *Céim: Standards for Initial Teacher Education in Ireland* identifies GCE as one of seven core elements that must underpin all aspects of teacher education programmes (Teaching Council, 2020, p.14). Thus, it is expected that all future educators will integrate into their teaching new value-based knowledge, skills and attitudes that seek to build a more peaceful, just and sustainable world. In effect (and affect), this authenticates the importance of continually working on one's 'self', as well as with Others, in these evermore 'disruptive' times.

To commit to GCE, therefore, is to engage in some form of struggle. Drawing on Socratic wisdom, this may be necessary to advance oneself and one's practices. This struggle need not be overly burdensome, however – indeed, it may lead to new creative and enjoyable learning experiences. In this way, GCE promotes a range of affirming pedagogical practices. Specifically, GCE inspires educators to become more at ease with:

- Asking questions, however 'contentious' (Hess & McAvoy, 2014);
- Exploring diverse viewpoints and values;
- Making new inter-connections at global-local levels;
- Responding as active global citizens; and
- Embracing more holistic approaches to assessment (Oxfam, 2015).

Practically, there are a myriad of resources available to help educators teach more inclusively and creatively, including links with: Irish Aid, Oxfam, Irish Development Education Authority (IDEA), World Wise Global Schools (WWGS), Global Action Plan, and The Ubuntu Network, amongst others. Perhaps the most valuable resource, however, are the educators themselves whose newfound attitudes and practices can foster greater learning enjoyment (Noddings, 2003) and can help learners "to travel together differently in a foggy road – with the stamina for the long-haul rather than a desire for quick fixes" (Andreotti *et al.*, 2018, p.17). While it may be challenging for educators to become comfortable with (and prepared for) co-engaging with diverse learners (Hagan & McGlynn, 2004; Conway *et al.*, 2011; O'Brien & Cotter, 2018), there are methodological supports on how to teach differently, for different purposes and with different learners in mind. This involves the use of participatory, innovative and active learning methods (Ladson-Billings, 2009; Leonardo, 2009). This involves practising authentic democratic experiences and committing to the critical act of teaching (Freire, 1996; Giroux, 2020). And this involves courageous experimentation and risk-taking, which enables educators and learners to learn and 'unlearn' together (Simpson, 2019).

It may take a particular kind of educator to do GCE work well. But this person is never complete and is always 'in the making'. Freire reminds us that it is only through self-experience in the world that we may become who we are (Freire, 1996); and that only by seeking to nurture our own values of mutual respect, care, vulnerability, courage and solidarity, can we become better human beings (Freire, 2014; Hoy, 2024). Accordingly, in the act of empowering ourselves, we begin the journey of empowering Others.

How to Use this Book

This *Handbook* has been created with a view to supporting teachers to practise core aspects of GCE. We offer some guidance on discussion and exploration of GCE-related themes, practice of praxis methods, how to engage in reflective habits and take action (as teachers) in your post-primary classroom setting. We, the authors, are also educators and are aware of all the demands which teaching places on you. To this end, we have included a few suggestions on how to get the most out of this *Handbook*, which include:

- How to use conceptual understandings to guide and develop your practice as a teacher of GCE;
- Timing;
- Preparing your own collection of resources; and
- Funding opportunities to help you raise awareness and visibility of GCE concerns in your learning community.

This *Handbook* provides you with a conceptual framework to help develop your own understanding of why this work is so important and how your own identity, both personally and professionally, is foundational to developing your practice. In each lesson, we seek to explain some foundational theory of GCE and praxis as well as provide some useful questions, resources and tools which we hope, in time, will develop your own confidence as you practise GCE teaching. Throughout the lessons, we discuss leading theorists in the area of Critical Pedagogy, GCE, and praxis who have made the development of teaching resources possible. It is very valuable to connect to the conceptual framework in order to see the importance of why and how we implement various topics and methods at ground level – in our classrooms and schools.

Use the guidance at the beginning of each lesson to help you to reflect and plan your lessons, allow the ideas to sit with you and return to them to support your everyday teaching and learning. Perhaps you could start your own journal, fill it with questions and ponderings and your own suggestions.

This is a flexible curriculum framework. We have provided a structure to the *Handbook* which builds one lesson upon the next, so there is a flow and a progression in terms of topic and building understanding. Although we suggest following the lessons sequentially, we also invite you to be flexible with the time you spend on each lesson. The reality of life in the post-primary classroom is that each class group is different; there are often other demands; there are some groups who will converse and debate more than others and some who will require additional time for reflection; and projects created by different groups often take different lengths of time to put into action. We trust you, the teacher, to make your own professional choices; you know your own students best after all! We do suggest that each lesson should average between 90 and 120 minutes; however, we also invite you to stay flexible and responsive to the needs and interests of the learners around you.

In relation to resources, we know the practical reality of the school environment: the queues for the printer, the shortage of paper, the many unavoidable malfunctions! So, we suggest you make your own pack by laminating the resources. Having laminated materials means the learners can move pieces about in activities, and in the long run you spend less time cutting and organising. You can have a file of resources which you may use any time with this *Handbook*, or indeed with different groups – not to mention, laminating these resources is an environmentally conscious act!

Some very useful resources have been included in the **References** so please use them, create your own resources, and share. This community of practice is central to the ethos of GCE as we support and collaborate in solidarity.

If you require more funding, then we suggest that you go online to https://www.worldwiseschools.ie/grants/ and apply for grant funding to support your practice. Also, why not elevate the visibility of your fine work by applying for a Global Passport at https://www.worldwiseschools.ie/global-passport/?

Final Words

This text is one of a myriad of GCE resources 'out there' for teachers. It is so encouraging to see the materialisation of GCE work that provides foundational, evidence-based and heuristic guidelines for teachers. Internationally, we may look here, for example, to Oxfam's (2015) publication, *Global Citizenship in the Classroom: A guide for teachers*. In an Irish context, there are wonderful examples of innovative, practice-based, scholarship happening – to name but a few, Campbell *et al.* (2023), Dolan (Ed., 2024) and Golden (Ed., 2024). Our *Handbook* is but one step amongst many on the journey for further GCE knowledge and experience.

In advance of practising and reviewing the lessons in this *Handbook*, you may find it useful to research more widely in the field. You also may find it useful to preview our mini video series which serves as a useful accompaniment to this Handbook (see Hoy & O'Brien, 2022; Donnelly, Hoy &

O'Brien, 2023). The first of these videos provides a further introduction to the principles and values of GCE, while the second presents first-hand insights into student teachers' experiences of doing GCE work in the classroom.

Independently, we hope you find this *Handbook* to be both informative and enjoyable. We hope that its lessons may inspire further dialogue with your students and peers. Your GCE work with your students is needed more than ever. As this book goes to print, the world is ever-more troubled by climate change, wars and military conflicts, forced migration, global ill-heath and inequality, human rights violations, extremism and the exponential rise in intolerance towards others. The United Nations *2030 Agenda* and the Sustainable Development Goals (SDGs) direct us towards actions that seek out greater peace and prosperity on this planet. While achieving these worthy goals remains uncertain, education plays a key, more localised, role in their realisation. Education fosters critical scholarship. Education nurtures active citizenry. And education offers us all hope for the future.

We wish you well with your own important GCE work in the classroom.

Seánín Hoy, Gearóid O'Brien & Stephen O'Brien

Do your little bit of good where you are; it's those little bits of good put together that overwhelm the world.

BISHOP DESMOND TUTU

LESSON 1:
GLOBAL CITIZENSHIP EDUCATION

Global Citizenship Education (GCE) is a term which is starting to appear more and more in school life and school curricula. With the introduction of the *Céim* standards that presents GCE as one of seven core teacher competences, we can expect to see more integration of GCE-related issues in the post-primary classroom. It is important, therefore, for young people to explore what GCE means, what the core values and attitudes of GCE and a praxis curriculum are, and what knowledge and skills they can expect to develop in the (praxis-oriented) classroom where GCE is enacted.

GCE is an expansive field of study, covering many areas of learning (some of which will be explored throughout this *Handbook*). It is important to establish a sense of sharing ideas right from the beginning, communicating to the students in the classroom that, in the GCE space, we want to activate prior knowledge, acknowledge multiple perspectives and signal that this is a space of active learning. The opening activities in this lesson invite learners to puzzle over various ideas and themes connected with GCE, including their own contextual experiences of this term. We hope that this enables the teacher (who may or may not have experience in teaching GCE) to feel more comfortable in the knowledge that *they too* are nurturing alongside the evolving understandings of students.

Let's begin by taking a look at Irish Aid's definition for GCE. This serves as a useful (and superordinate) definition, encompassing as it does Development Education (DE) and Education for Sustainable Development (ESD):

> **Development education is a lifelong educational process which aims to increase public awareness and understanding of the rapidly changing, interdependent and unequal world in which we live. By challenging stereotypes and encouraging independent thinking, development education helps people to critically explore how global justice issues interlink with their everyday lives. Informed and engaged citizens are best placed to address complex social, economic and environmental issues linked to development. Development education empowers people to analyse, reflect on and challenge at a local and global level, the root causes and consequences of global hunger, poverty, injustice, inequality and climate change; presenting multiple perspectives on global justice issues.**
> (Irish Aid, 2017, p.6).

Guidance

Establishing a space where active learning and reflective thinking happens is crucial to establishing an effective praxis classroom. A praxis classroom is one – developed from the ideas of Paulo Freire – where people come together through dialogue to critically reflect on their reality and *transform* it through further action and reflection (a constant action-reflection process emerges). In this introductory lesson, we begin with activities which signal to the learners that everyone participates, everyone has a voice and a perspective and that we aim to share all these perspectives. Teaching critical thinking skills and reflective thinking habits work best when activated with the prior knowledge of the learners, when we listen to their own understandings and contextual experiences.

Andreotti *et al.* (2018) have created a tool which can be used to address local and global injustice issues with the objective of enacting change. The purpose of the tool is to help people identify and critically question commonly-held beliefs about issues such as 'development', poverty and wealth and, from this questioning, support them to effect local and global change. **Table 1.1** is based around the acronym HEADS UP. Included also is a list of questions/key considerations for the teacher practising GCE in the classroom.

In addition, there are nine core educational principles recently published by the Irish Government in the *Global Citizenship Education Strategy for 2021-2025* (IDEA, 2021) which can help you critically inform your lessons. These include:

- Knowledge;
- Root causes;
- Explicit ethos of GCE;
- Critical thinking;
- Participatory and creative methodologies;
- Quality resources and materials;
- Democratic skills;
- Creative thinking; and
- Reflective practice.

From the *GCE Strategy 2021-2025* (IDEA, 2021), we have provided in **Table 1.2** an example of a checklist that may help you when planning (this may also serve as a means of reflection during/after teaching a lesson).

You also may reflect upon how you, as the teacher, are learning each time you teach and that your willingness to engage in this work can inspire others. In the words of Miles Horton and Paulo Freire, "we make the road by walking" (Horton & Freire, 1990, p.3).

In the exercises contained in this lesson, the aim is to develop young people's awareness of how interconnected and interdependent we are in the world and to grapple with global justice issues, recognising that these issues have both local and global implications.

Table 1.1: The HEADS UP Tool
(adapted for use in the post-primary classroom)

Problematic (commonly-held) beliefs	Questions for the teacher to reflect on
Hegemony - leadership or dominance, especially by one state or social group over others	Do the texts we use, for example, represent multiple cultures? Do the students have agency in the classroom? Can they share their thoughts and ideas? Do we give more value or credit to some accounts than to others? Why?
Ethnocentrism - evaluation of other cultures according to preconceptions originating in the standards and customs of one's own culture	How do we make assumptions about what is 'normal' or natural, desirable or undesirable, moral or immoral? Do we compare Others in a negative light and/or in relation to our own situation or experience?
Ahistoricism	How do we make time to look at how history has impacted social, historical and economic spheres of society (and continues to do so)?
Depoliticisation	How do we explore issues such as Identity, Making Assumptions and Power in the classroom? How do we address and critique power disequilibrium in the classroom? Why is this important? Do we make space to hear marginalised voices and practise sharing multiple perspectives?
Self-congratulatory and self-serving attitudes	How are marginalised voices represented? How do we enable student voice and the sharing of student experiences in the classroom? How do we transition from a 'charity' stance to a 'solidarity' stance? How do we develop the skill of *empathy* and avoid ideas of 'pity' and/or 'white saviour' narratives?
Uncomplicated solutions	How do we prepare for and provide opportunities to learn about complex real-world issues? How do we think critically about the *root causes* of local and global injustices? How do we act to *change* the issues that concern us?
Paternalism	How are traditionally marginalised groups represented? How is paternalism present in modern education?

Table 1.2: GCE Teaching Checklist

Core Principle	Ways to implement in the lesson	Example
Knowledge	Make the classroom a place where there is a "mutual pursuit for knowledge" (hooks, 2010, p.159). Creating knowledge together begins with posing a problem and resisting the provision of a quick solution.	Have I posed a problem? For example, 'How do we rely on each other around the world?' Have I asked questions to inspire critical thinking? For example, 'How have you relied on others locally and globally since you woke up this morning?'
Root causes	Pose a problem and practise generating questions as a group to explore how that problem began.	Have I explored various strategies that lend themselves to generating questions? For example, 'Have I used the why-why-why chain activity?' [see **Worksheet 1.4**].
Explicit ethos of GCE	Place values at the core of everything you do and want to achieve in this learning space.	For example, 'Am I nurturing an environment that is respectful?' or 'Do we have a class charter where we can all express our wants and needs to make the class a place where everyone's right to learn and to teach are respected?'
Critical thinking	Ask and don't tell. Pose a problem and look at it together.	For example, 'Does everyone feel comfortable asking questions?' or 'Am I providing adequate time and space for students to consider the problem?' or 'What praxis strategies would support this?'
Participatory and creative methodologies	Everyone creates and participates in the class. Methods include working together in groups, questioning, dialogue, exploring, researching, developing awareness in self and sharing awareness with others in the school.	For example, 'What are the learners doing in class?' or 'What creative activities have I planned that enable them to learn about the topic?'
Quality resources and materials	Pool and share resources, adapt them and share them once more. GCE is about the development of a learning community – join one or create one.	For example, 'Do we have a school drive folder for GCE resources?' or 'Have I contacted WWGS (World Wise Global Schools) or another CSO (Civil Society Organisation) to receive CPD (Continuing Professional Development) training?' or 'Have I created resources and shared them?'
Democratic skills	Invitation of multiple perspectives. All learners (teacher and students) participate in creating knowledge and in decision-making processes.	For example, 'Is our learning space one that invites all learners to participate and share their perspectives?' or 'Do the students have agency?' or 'Are multiple perspectives represented in the texts I have used?'
Creative thinking	Possibility thinking – imagining education 'otherwise' (Andreotti, 2006).	For example, 'Do we encourage one another to be hopeful by imagining alternative ways to live together?'
Reflective practice	Routinely think about actions, attitudes, behaviours and values. Practise getting comfortable with questioning ourselves.	For example, 'Is reflective practice regular and ongoing in our class?' or 'Do we give it the time it deserves?' or 'Have I planned for regular 'step-back' moments where we can think about what we are learning?'

This introductory lesson initiates a collaborative investigation of root causes of global injustices as young people, alongside their teacher, ask questions and help one another to make connections between global (and local) injustices. The teacher can take this opportunity to develop understanding by asking questions as the connection web game plays out. For example, 'How can we eliminate global poverty?', 'Where does it begin and why?', 'Who is responsible for global poverty?', etc. A helpful guide may be to consider questions that begin with 'how' and 'why'. Creating a classroom atmosphere that welcomes questions is really important. Further, it is not the sole responsibility of the teacher to question – to develop a shared learning environment that centres on the development of critical literacy, the teacher *guides* by questioning, modelling and encouraging students to generate their own questions.

Activities

The purpose of the introductory exercise in this lesson is to share initial understandings of what GCE means and what types of topics/knowledge arenas can be explored therein. This is useful as it enables students to see that their ideas are both welcome and valid and that their participation is both expected and encouraged.

In getting feedback from students, it is important to focus on how they have developed their own understanding on GCE and global themes. We are looking for changes in knowledge, skills, attitudes and values. The teacher can also enquire about learning engagement/enjoyment – 'What activities did the students enjoy and why?'. In your questioning try to focus on why they have been drawn to certain issues, how global and local issues are connected, and how we are all connected. You can pause and further discuss the concept of 'interconnectedness' and/or 'interdependence'. To help young people further their understanding of these terms you can use the second activity, which is inspired by a quote from Martin Luther King. This activity helps young people to link their own contexts, their own everyday experiences, with others around the world. This is a great way to initiate conversations about connectedness, power and, indeed, exploitation. Young people can learn about how the decisions which are made in one place can impact people living on the other side of the world. We are thus all interconnected. Global interdependence also looks at how the most affluent countries in the world depend on the riches of other countries, from food items to minerals and other abstract or 'soft' commodities such as knowledge and culture.

The next task of this introductory lesson requires some space, so push back the chairs or, where possible, find a larger space or even go outside. A few practicalities need to be taken care of. You may need to print the 'suggested issues for connection web' (see **Worksheet 1.3**). We suggest printing these individually on A4 paper (two per page works well) and laminating them for future use. Space the issues around the room or learning arena and invite students to choose one that they are drawn to. The students will later explain to the group why they chose this issue specifically and will then connect their chosen issue with someone else's chosen issue, all the while explaining why they believe they are interconnected. This is a wonderful exercise that enables students to be at the centre of their learning. Beyond this, it provides an opportunity to communicate and to genuinely feel a change in who has power, expertise, agency in the GCE learning space. Here we are physically in a circle, sharing thoughts, ideas and questions. The teacher is in the circle alongside the students. No one person is in control or has authority. This is a powerful and meaningful observation for all to make in the introductory lesson and it is a way for you, the teacher, to feel more comfortable with changing the traditional dynamics of the classroom.

In the closing task of this lesson, choose one of the themes you have introduced and invite the students to work in groups to explore the root causes of the theme. You could, depending on your group, allocate a different theme or, even better, invite students to choose a theme. For example, if climate change is the theme, invite the students to provide reasons for 'why' climate change is an issue, and what causes it? This could lead to answers such as 'pollution' and 'deforestation'. Then invite the students to consider the reasons why pollution and deforestation are issues in the world. Perhaps students will comment on industrialisation, excessive transport use, etc. You can keep the why-why-why chain going as long as the students are able, and you could provide access to the Internet so they can research their issue. The main idea is to encourage the students to generate questions and embed critical thinking habits in the learning space.

Another exercise you could use in this introductory lesson is to ask the students to look at the following problem: 'North African people are forced to leave their homes', watch the following news report (YouTube video, https://youtu.be/QLCFD0pVfN8, Refugees flee conflict sparked by climate change in Central Africa, *PBS Newshour*, 8 minutes, 59 seconds) and record any details which explain why these people have no choice but to leave their homes. The video should help to engage students. They can watch the video for ideas and then translate these ideas into the why-why-why activity.

Reflection

In the reflective element of this lesson, it is important to consider the key themes/issues of both global and local concern, as well as inviting the learners to consider how these issues might involve them. Exploring what justice and injustice means is very important in this initial stage too. When examining the GCE themes suggested, you may pose questions that relate to why these global issues are in fact 'injustice' issues. You may then invite the group(s) to reflect on who is treated unfairly and by whom, as well as discuss why they are being treated unfairly.

Lesson Plan 1: Global Citizenship Education

Purpose of this lesson (learning objectives):
To share prior knowledge and/or experience of GCE and related 'glocal' themes.

Teacher Materials:
- A3 paper
- Pens for sharing
- KWL charts – see https://www.educatorstechnology.com/wp-content/uploads/2023/06/6-Ways-to-Use-KWL-Charts-with-Students.png
- A long piece of string
- Words/Issues listed here cut up
- Space (consideration to seating and space for movement)

Format:
Flexible group learning

	Activity	Let's talk about it
Lead in What is GCE?	In groups, invite students to write down anything they know or think they know about GCE. Read out the Irish Aid definition. Write KWL on a white board and gather students' thoughts and ideas.	What do you already know about GCE? What would you like to know?
Movable pieces activity	Invite the class to look at the words on **Worksheet 1.1** and decide which ones best describe GCE.	Which word or words stand out to you? Why? Would you include all of these definitions? Why/why not?
How are we dependent on one another?	Invite the class to read the quote from Dr. Martin Luther King, Jr. on **Worksheet 1.2**. Then ask them to write down all the things they have done from the moment they opened their eyes to the moment they arrive at school. This is a good activity to do using the Think-Pair-Share method.	In groups, consider all the things you have done before arriving at school: every little thing. Think and jot down what you did. Share your notes with the person beside you. Now consider how you have depended on others around the world. For example: How did you wake up? Was it your phone alarm? Where did the components of your phone come from?

	Activity	Let's talk about it
The Connection Web activity	Using **Worksheet 1.3**, spread cut up issues around the floor. Ask students each to choose their issue. Form a circle where everyone holds up an issue so the group can see. One by one, invite participants to share: 1. The reason why they chose the word/issue 2. Find another word in the room that they think their word connects to and why – the string is then passed to them. The game continues until everyone is connected by the piece of string. Ask everyone who has a word/phrase that is 'counter' development (like 'child labour' or 'climate change', for example) to sit down. The participants will feel the strain on the string. Explain that this is symbolic of the strain the world is under when all of these issues are affecting us. **Worksheet 1.3** offers suggested issues, but this activity can be adapted to add any other relevant issue.	Why did you choose that word? What do you already know? What would you like to know? Why did you choose the other word to connect to?

	Activity	Let's talk about it
The Why-why-why Chain activity	The purpose of this activity (**Worksheet 1.4**) is to help students to generate their own questions and to explore root causes. Explain and model the task for the students. Here is a YouTube video (https://youtu.be/R5NAb1GRoPk, *Methodologies for Global Citizenship* [2.14 mins]) to watch beforehand to understand how the activity works. You could use this activity for any of the lessons but it could be a very useful way to explore root causes of how someone becomes a refugee/asylum seeker or displaced person. You can refer to this website (https://separatedchild.org/our-work/child-refugee-stories/) to get some ideas for guiding such activities based on true stories from children who had been separated from their families whilst trying to flee their home countries. One of the themes explored in the connection web is forced migration. Take some time to explore the root causes of this problem. On the white board, work through the first set of exploratory questions alongside the students. Once the students have actively listened and watched the video, they will be positioned to answer these questions and then generate their own. Here is a video link for 'North African people are forced to leave their homes' (https://www.youtube.com/watch?v=QLCFD0pVfN8).	**Issue:** I drove through a red light. *Why?* Late for work. *Why?* Woke up late. *Why?* Alarm clock didn't go off. *Why?* Forgot to set it last night. *Why?* Was really tired and fell asleep. *Why?* Had a busy day. *Why?* Son was ill. *Why?* He had an asthma attack. *Why?* Hay-fever. *Why?* ... **Issue:** A child is alone in a strange country. *Why?* Lost his family. *Why?* They drowned at sea. *Why?* They fell off a crowded boat. *Why?* There were too many people and the boat could not carry them safely. *Why?* So many people needed to escape. *Why?* They were being persecuted. *Why?* ... **Issue:** North African people are forced to leave their homes. *Why?* Failed farming. *Why?* Parched lands. *Why?* Land exploitation.

Time to think

Why are these themes/issues both a global and local concern?
How do they involve you?
Why are these issues 'injustice' issues? Who is being treated unfairly? By whom?

Worksheet 1.1: Movable Pieces activity

Involves asking questions and critical thinking	Involves exploring local-global connections and our views, values and assumptions	Involves providing simple solutions to complex issues	Involves (only) about far-away places and peoples
Involves the whole-school environment	Involves telling people what to think and do	Involves a strong focus on charity	Involves exploring the complexity of global issues and engaging with multiple perspectives
Involves exploring issues of social justice locally and globally	Involves tokenistic inclusion of learners in decision-making	Involves no connection to real life events	Involves all areas of the curriculum
Involves learning in the classroom only	Involves applying learning to real-world issues and contexts	Involves making things too difficult for young children to understand	Involves being a stand-alone extra subject
Involves enrichment of everyday teaching and learning	Involves being the focus for a specific day or week (not every day)	Involves opportunities for learners to take informed, reflective action and have their voices heard	Involves all ages

Interconnected Activity adapted from *Oxfam Global Citizenship Teacher Guide*
https://oxfamilibrary.openrepository.com/bitstream/handle/10546/620105/edu-global-citizenship-teacher-guide-091115-en.pdf;sequence=9

Worksheet 1.2: Dr. Martin Luther King, Jr.

"Before you finish eating breakfast this morning, you've depended on more than half the world."

DR. MARTIN LUTHER KING, Jr.

Source: Oxfam (2015). *Global Citizenship in the Classroom: A Guide for Teachers*, p.6.

Worksheet 1.3: Suggested Issues for the Connection Web Activity

Aid	Community
Trade	Emergency
Child Labour	Income
Climate Change	Food
Food security	Globalisation
Gender	Debt
Equality	Deforestation
War	Distribution of Wealth
Corruption	History
Governance	Exploitation
HIV and AIDS	micro-credit
Malaria	Sustainable energy
Natural disasters	Health
Population	Shelter
Migration	Colonisation
Human rights	United Nations
Quality education	Literacy
Access to education	Sweat-shops
Disability	Oil
Water and sanitation	Interdependence
Livelihood	Power
Capacity-building	Peace
Religious persecution	Indigenous peoples

Source: Connection Web activity adapted from WWGS//; www.worldwiseschools.ie/resource-library/.

Worksheet 1.4: The Why-Why-Why Chain activity

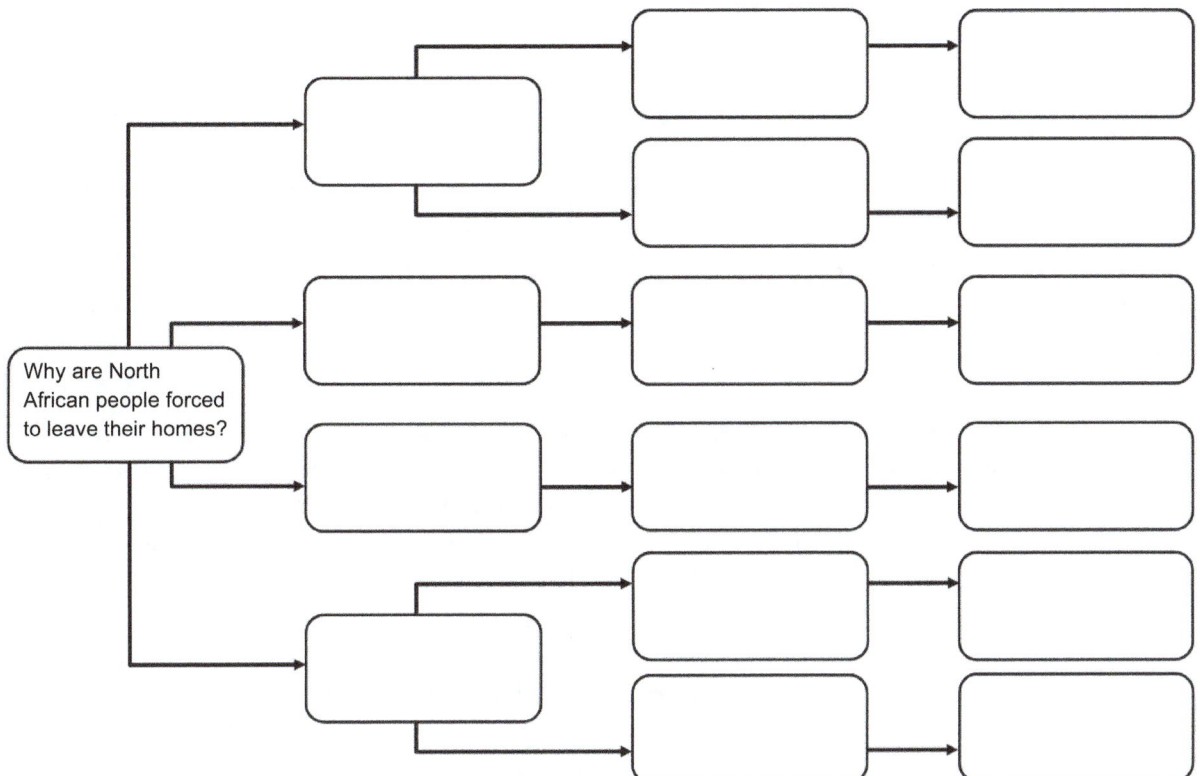

Follow the Why-why-why chain through for the question above – or for an example provided.

Source: The Why Why Why Chain Activity- resource adapted from
https://www.oxfam.org.uk/education/classroom-resources

LESSON 2: EXPLORING OUR OWN IDENTITY

Before we explore the importance of the lesson on identity, consider the extract below from the inspiring book, *Women Who Run with the Wolves*, by Clarissa Pinkola Estés. It encapsulates the importance of identity and how names or identities can simultaneously empower and cause destruction. In this *Handbook*, there are lessons that reinforce the beauty of identity and the wholesome nature of identity as it provides us with a sense of home, belonging and togetherness. At the same time, later in the *Handbook*, you have the opportunity to explore how being labelled 'asylum seeker', for example, can eliminate your sense of who you are, can reinforce isolation and strip you of your sense of home and belonging again and again.

Estés writes:

Naming a force, creature, person, or thing has several connotations. In cultures where names are chosen carefully for their magical or auspicious meanings, to know a person's true name means to know the life path and the soul attributes of that person. And the reason the true name is often kept secret is to protect the owner of the name so that he or she [or they] might grow into the power of the name, to shelter it so that no one will either denigrate it or distract from it, and so that one's spiritual authority can develop to its full proportions. (Estés, 2008, p.118)

Guidance

This lesson focuses on 'personal identity'. As young people begin to explore their own identity, they will begin to recognise commonalities they share with others as well as their own uniqueness. You can draw their attention to Article 1 of the United Nations' *Universal Declaration of Human Rights*, which states that every person is "born free and equal in dignity and rights" regardless of "nationality, place of residence, sex, national or ethnic origin, colour, religion, language, or any other status" (United Nations, 1948).

Exploring identity is a powerful, transformative and ethical teaching practice. It is a theme that lends itself to many different pedagogies and an entry point into the established post-primary curriculum. Learning about the importance of identity enables all learners (both students and teachers alike) to begin this exploration within ourselves, with our own understandings, assumptions, prejudices and contexts. It is important to begin deep and meaningful learning with sharing of our own personal experiences and perspectives. We are drawn to the quote from Estés' well-acclaimed book because it invites us to consider how our identities are formed and are formative to others. In exploring our identities, we feel the ground again with bare feet, taking notice of the paths we have walked, are walking and will walk. We practise paying closer attention to ourselves and to others and, by doing so, we also practise respect and empathy.

Activities

This lesson on 'Identity' is an opportunity to invite young people to activate their own knowledge about identity, begin with who they are and the different parts that make them who they are. This may be an opportunity for some students to share their personal or family cultures, their gender identities, their ethnic background or birthplace. The lesson can be fun and creative and also a celebration of difference and diversity in the classroom. Essentially, however, it is a crucial foundation for the lessons that follow.

Its purpose is to establish where the pupils' understanding of the concept of identity lies and, from this starting point, to begin to explore the multiple connotations of identity. We want to encourage pupils to critically consider their identities and explore how revealing pieces of your identity can lead to behaviours that exclude. It is also an opportunity to discuss and reflect upon how some identities receive privilege over others – for example, when we look at dominant religions or races in Irish schools or when a student who speaks English as their first language may not think of language as being an important part of their identity, whilst others who speak English as a second language may be very aware of this aspect. Students can take time to consider why this may be so and this can be a very real, relevant entry point into discussion about privilege.

Table 2.1 offers various aspects of identity that you can use to probe and question.

Table 2.1: Aspects of Identity

Aspects of Identity	Discussion topics
Ethnicity	Identities you think about most often
Socio-economic status	Identities you think about least often
Gender	Your own identities you would like to know more about
Sex	
Sexual orientation	Identities that have the strongest effect on how you perceive yourself
National origin	Identities that have the greatest effect on how others perceive you.
First language	
Physical, emotional, developmental (dis)ability	
Age	
Religious or spiritual affiliation	
Race	

Source: Adapted from a resource on the Social Identity Wheel: https://sites.lsa.umich.edu/inclusive-teaching/personal-identity-wheel/.

You should discuss what words such as 'family', 'background', 'civil status', 'gender', 'sexual orientation' and 'ethnicity' entail, remembering to start with the students' own understandings and asking questions to build upon this foundation. Here are some examples of how you can approach this:

- Let's jot down everything we associate with family, background and ethnicity. There are no right or wrong answers. Just write down what comes to mind.
- When someone asks you what your background is, what do you think they mean?
- Under which category do you think you might find civil status, etc?

It is also important here to ask why the sample ID cards (**Worksheet 2.1**) are different? Why have people provided different pieces of information about themselves? It is valuable to have group discussions about how we often choose to reveal some things about ourselves and not others.

As the facilitator, it is important to know that lessons about identity can have challenges. For example, learners sitting close together may be able to see each other's ID cards and some learners may feel some vulnerability about aspects of their identity which are invisible to others. We suggest full disclosure at the beginning that whatever the learners choose to share is their decision. Also by keeping discussion questions broad, learners are given the opportunity to share or keep private.

Lesson Plan 2: Exploring Our Own Identity

Purpose of this lesson (learning objectives):
To explore the concept of Identity

Learning Objectives:
By the end of this lesson, it is expected that students will be able to:
- Identify aspects of their personal identity;
- Discuss with others those aspects of their identity that are important to them;
- Identify how their own and another's identity might be similar and/or different;
- Have a greater appreciation of the uniqueness of each other.

Teacher Materials:
- A2 and A3 paper
- pens for sharing
- KWL Charts
- Template for Personalised ID (**Worksheet 2.2**)
- Space (consideration to seating and space for movement)

Format:
Flexible group learning

	Activity	Let's talk about it
Lead in **Establish students' prior understanding of identity**	Provide large pages and pens to students in groups, invite them to write down in three minutes as many things as possible that they associate with the word 'identity'. Emphasise that there are no right or wrong answers.	What do you already know about 'identity'? Why is it important? What questions do you have about identity?
Personal Identity Cards exercise	Invite students to go on an imaginary journey …. When they arrive at their destination, there is no guarantee even they will know themselves so they must create their own personalised ID (**Worksheet 2.2** – see Worksheet **2.1.** as examples but feel free to make your own).	Consider: <ul><li>What are the types of aspects of you which make you unique?</li><li>What pieces of yourself would you want to hold on to and remember?</li></ul>

Time to think
What have you noticed? What have you learned about identity? If anyone would like to share their identity card information, encourage the students to share. The teacher can also participate and share their identity card and invite students to compare their cards with the teachers. Are there any similarities or differences?

Worksheet 2.1: Personalised ID Activity

Imagine ...

You are about to be transported into the future – but there is no guarantee that, when you arrive, you will know yourself.

Therefore, each of you has been given the opportunity to create your own personalised ID.

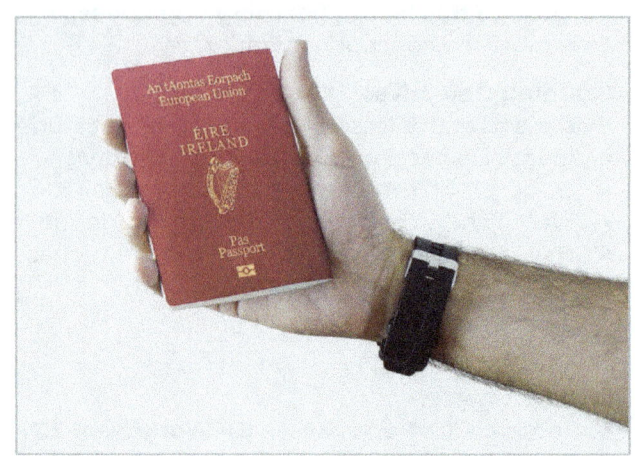

Look at these examples:

Name	James Parkinson
Date of birth	May 1985
Place of birth	Longford
Family	Not married; one sister; parents dead
Occupation	Games programmer, working from home
Background	B.Sc. in IT
Interests	Computer languages, AI
Other	Walking

Name	Eileen O'Neill
Date of birth	July 1989
Place of birth	Halting site, Co. Kerry
Family	Husband, Liam, and two daughters
Occupation	Public representative
Background	LCA student; BA in Community Development
Interests	Working with marginalised groups; Family and community; Introducing Traveller culture & history to the school curriculum
Other	Fluent Irish; Reading

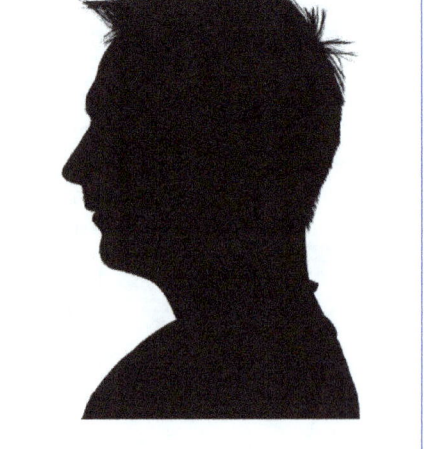

Name	Emily Cusack
Date of birth	August 1993
Place of birth	Londonderry
Family	Partner, Niamh, and two dogs
Occupation	Marketing manager, food company
Background	Worked in catering company after school, was quickly promoted to management; some evening courses on food and management
Interests	Food! Seeing marketing campaigns succeed.
Other	Visited 25 European countries – working on the rest!

Name	Donal MacFlaherty
Date of birth	December 2007
Place of birth	Dublin
Family	Parents, two younger brothers
Occupation	Professional footballer
Background	Local GAA; currently playing with Bohs – looking for move to the UK
Interests	All sports
Other	Restoring an old Jag my Dad bought – he says it's mine once it's mobile!

Name	Felica Okbuswana
Date of birth	April 1996
Place of birth	Ogun State, Nigeria
Family	No family in Ireland
Occupation	Nursing assistant
Background	Came to Ireland as asylum-seeker at 7; 6 years in Direct Provision; working and training to become a qualified nurse
Interests	Poetry – and how it impacts people
Other	Music

Worksheet 2.2: My Personal Identity Card

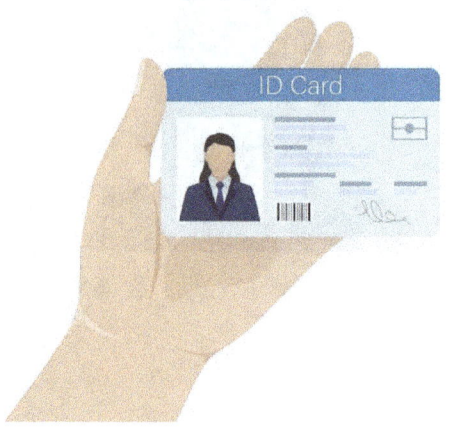

My Personal Identity Card

NAME	
BORN	
AGE	
FAMILY	
BACKGROUND	
RELIGION	
GENDER	
INTERESTS	
OTHER	

Source: Adapted from 'Spotlight on stereotyping - a resource for teachers: https://www.developmenteducation.ie/media/documents/Spotlight-on-Stereotyping.pdf

LESSON 3:
I AM FROM ...

Inviting learners to engage in artistic expressions of identity is a very helpful method in terms of enabling confidence and varying levels of a sharing of personal stories. The creative tasks will invite a plurality of voices, expressions and cultural experiences, whilst also promoting holistic literacy in the classroom. Central to the ethos of GCE are community and inclusive values such as respect, diversity, empathy, and identity. Andreotti (2006, p.29) explains how we enact change "from the inside to the outside'" and how the central principles for this transformation are predicated upon questioning one's own assumptions and by becoming reflexive practitioners. In exploring themes such as Identity, we can encourage respect for the diversity of existence which naturally permeates our classrooms and wider communities.

Guidance

Exploring Identity is crucial in laying the foundations for exploring discrimination, for exploring belonging and home/homelessness. When learners can discuss and experience the importance of identity, there is potential for a deeper understanding of what happens to a person when their identity is taken from them, when their identity is given to them, and when their identity is 'deconstructed' (Olusanya, 2021). In Felicia Olusanya's (*ibid.*) spoken word poem about the experience of living in Direct Provision, she describes how such centres strip away your identity. This is a powerful and incredibly meaningful poem and when you come to this activity in the *Handbook*, it is crucial to have laid the foundations so students can fully understand and relate to how much we stand to lose when our identity is taken away from us.

Activities

In this lesson, we build upon developing this awareness again. Young people can connect with the layers of meaning behind our identities and our homes. By exploring these ideas through creative writing, young people can begin to feel an emotional connection to these big concepts. We suggest that you join in with the group, make your own poem and share something of your choice from your own life or background.

You might begin by reading the poem by poet and activist Mary Pipher (**Worksheet 3.1**). When she herself engaged in research with a group of refugees, she invited them to write 'I am From...' poetry. Pipher comments on how this self-writing is a useful way to explore a range of identity issues – writing comes from our existence and it has the power to teach us who we are:

If you look back on your life, most likely you will be able to trace a trail from the present to deep in your past. Pivotal events shaped your core values. Certain people and experiences interested you. You had talents and ways you spent your time. Most likely, you cared about certain things – school, sports, animals, politics, religion. The trail into your past may be linear or meandering, or at some point, it may have taken a sharp right turn. (Pipher, 2007, p.34)

Once you have read the poem through with the other learners, you can offer an example of your own.

Next, using **Worksheet 3.2** as a prompt or template, ask students to write their own *I Am From...* poem. Young people enjoy being able to explore who they are and express themselves and this activity allows them to do just that. It is personal and some people will feel more at ease revealing personal stories, others will prefer to be more discreet; some will share and some may not choose to share. There is a sense of showing one's vulnerability in this lesson but there is no need to feel concerned. You might speak with your students and explain that, although participation (as always) is expected, sharing their poems or their prints is ultimately their choice. The display of the work is not the objective. The aim is to enable thinking, discussion, and reflection. This lesson grounds work in later lessons, as we develop discussions about loss of identity and home.

This is an evocative activity. Often learners feel quite sentimental and nostalgic throughout. Some students may struggle with completing the entire template, therefore encouraging learners to not overthink the exercise or (where willing) asking learners to share examples is helpful. Learners often can find it challenging to describe their own personality or a talent they have. Encourage them to ask another friend in the class or highlight something you have noticed about them or their abilities.

When the poems are completed, invite the learners to take their thumb prints. You can buy a fingerprint tool kit or alternatively paint can work too. The learners then examine their own unique print and sketch a larger version of their print to fill an A4 size page. It does not need to be precise, just something which resembles their print and the lines running through it. Show an example on the whiteboard (examples are provided in **Worksheet 3.3**). The learners can transfer their poems to the print on the A4 page. If the learners are happy to share their poems with one another, you could make a display on the wall of the classroom. Depending on your group, learners may be willing to read their poems and ask each other questions about the words they have chosen. **Table 3.1** offers some sample questions to generate good discussion:

Table 3.1: Discussion Questions

> Can you explain why you have chosen to include more than one city?
>
> Why is this place significant to you? What makes it special?
>
> Why did you choose this adjective to describe yourself?
>
> How do you celebrate this tradition with your family?
>
> Why is this holiday meaningful to you?
>
> Why do you find this activity enjoyable?
>
> Why are these smells significant to you? Do they remind you of something or someone?
>
> Can you tell us more about this experience?
>
> I also love this character, I love her because she is …. Why do you appreciate her?
>
> How does this make you laugh? Tell me more about this person who makes you laugh? Why is it so important to laugh?
>
> That is a powerful quote, what do you think the author/writer/singer is trying to say?
>
> Why does this make you feel proud?
>
> When did you first realise you had this talent?
>
> Why is this particular story meaningful to you?
>
> Tell me more about this person who said something that made you feel special.
>
> Why is it important to have ambitions?
>
> Why is it important to have hopes for the future? How do you intend to fulfil these hopes?

Reflection

This foundational learning is crucial. Later in the *Handbook* when you discuss loss of home and identity, and loss of self, you can return to these questions and poems and pose deeper questions. For example, you could ask how might someone, who loses their home or their identity, feel about losing all of these pieces of themselves? In building empathy, such development of understanding of what identity actually entails is vital. For example, when we try to understand how difficult it is for someone to start over in a new country, to seek asylum without being labelled 'an asylum seeker', to rebuild their identities and their lives.

Lesson Plan 3: I Am From …

Purpose of this lesson (learning objectives):
To explore the concept of Identity.

Learning Objectives:
By the end of this lesson, it is expected that:
- Students will learn about the author Mary Pipher and her poem, *I Am From* (**Worksheet 3.1**);
- Students will think critically and reflect to write a self-identity poem inspired by *I Am From*;
- Students will learn the meaning behind a fingerprint and its relation to identity by engaging in a short discussion and explanation;
- Students will create a design of their poem in the form of a fingerprint to reflect their uniqueness by using mixed media paper, stickers, markers, coloured pencils, and calligraphy pens.

Teacher Materials:
- A2 and A3 paper
- Pens for sharing
- KWL charts
- Ink pods or hand paint (to take thumbprint)
- Scissors
- Poem
- Template of poem (**Worksheet 3.2**)
- Space (consideration to seating and space for movement)

Format:
Flexible group learning

	Activity	Let's talk about it
Lead in **Establish students' prior understanding of identity**	Introduce and explain the poem, *I Am From*, and author Mary Pipher, as well as the content of the poem. Make a connection to the purpose of the lesson and activity. Invite students to read and/or listen to teacher recital of a poem, *I am From*, by Mary Pipher, *Writing to Change the World* (**Worksheet 3.1**).	Who are you? Where do you come from?
I Am From… poem activity	Explain to students the creation of own *I Am From* poem; students can follow example template (**Worksheet 3.2**) or individually brainstorm different ideas that can be incorporated into their poem.	
Fingerprinting activity	Start a short discussion regarding the meaning behind fingerprints in connection with identity. Explain fingerprint drawing for poem; students will print their own fingerprints in a separate Post-it and see an example to create own fingerprint poem (**Worksheet 3.3**).	

Time to think
Why might it be problematic asking someone "Where are you from?"

Worksheet 3.1: I Am From

I am from Avis and Frank, Agnes and Fred, Glessie May and Mark.

From the Ozark Mountains and the high plains of Eastern Colorado,

From mountain snowmelt and lazy southern creeks filled with water moccasins.

I am from oatmeal eaters, gizzard eaters, haggis and raccoon eaters.

I'm from craziness, darkness, sensuality, and humor.

From intense do-gooders struggling through ranch winters in the 1920s.

I'm from "If you can't say anything nice about someone don't say anything" and "Pretty is as pretty does" and "Shit-muckety brown" and "Damn it all to hell."

I'm from no-dancing-or-drinking Methodists, but cards were okay except on Sunday, and from tent-meeting Holy Rollers,

From farmers, soldiers, bootleggers, and teachers.

I'm from Schwinn girl's bike, 1950 Mercury two-door, and West Side Story.

I'm from coyotes, baby field mice, chlorinous swimming pools,

Milky Way and harvest moon over Nebraska cornfields.

I'm from muddy Platte and Republican,

From cottonwood and mulberry, tumbleweed and switchgrass

From Willa Cather, Walt Whitman, and Janis Joplin,

My own sweet dance unfolding against a cast of women in aprons and barefoot men in overalls.

Mary Pipher, *Writing to Change the World* (2006).

Worksheet 3.2: I Am From Sample Questions

I am from……………… *neighbourhood, town, city, country, state, continent.*

I am from……………… *a place with special meaning to you.*

I am from……………… *an important moment or recollection in your life.*

I am from……………… *your own personality.*

I am from……………… *a significant holiday or a tradition you share with others.*

I am from……………… *a food you love to eat or prepare or share with others.*

I am from……………… *a favourite childhood toy/your favourite colour.*

From……………… *activities you really love doing/favourite pastimes.*

From……………… *a smell that you love or that makes you remember someone or something.*

I am from……………… *a significant experience you have shared with others.*

I am from……………… *your favourite character from a novel or film/ favourite sporting activity.*

I am from……………… *something that makes you laugh loudly!*

From……………… *a quote that inspires you.*

I am from……………… *something you have said, done or achieved of which you are proud.*

I am from……………… *something special or unique about you.*

I am from……………… *something you care for deeply (another person or animal).*

I am from……………… *your favourite song or piece of music.*

From ……………… *words someone once said to you that you cherish.*

And ……………… *a dream, a hope or an ambition for your future or the future of the world.*

Worksheet 3.3: I Am from Fingerprints

LESSON 4:
HOME IS WHERE OUR HEARTS ARE

This lesson focuses on the importance of 'home'; how this concept creates for us a sense of belonging. Again, learners are engaged in co-constructing empathy, as they initiate discussions with their own experiences of home. Later, when they come to discuss the issue of homelessness, students may come to a more developed understanding of the *magnitude* of that loss.

Guidance

The lesson begins with an activity on 'belonging' whereby the students engage with the complexities surrounding the question: "Where do you come from?". In this lesson, young people have the opportunity to reflect on the different ways that this question can be interpreted; how it has the potential to exclude someone; and how it might be responded to differently.

Students are then introduced to two key ideas: Belonging and Not belonging. They are invited to think of words that they associate with both. In a group of learners with different mother tongues, this activity can be a lovely way to share language and cultural norms. Sharing other words from multiple languages, for example, really enriches this activity and enables every learner to actively contribute. Students can explain vocabulary and ideas that are specific to their own culture. For example, Spanish students may contribute '*pertenecer*'. which translates as 'belong'; German students may contribute '*sehnsucht*' which loosely translates as 'yearning'; a Brazilian student may share the Portuguese term '*saudades*', which means to 'yearn for someone or something', etc.

In the GCE classroom, sharing multiple perspectives is a central practice and the various contributions give so much depth to our understanding of a concept, which is not so readily captured by a single language term and/or idea. This invitation to use multiple languages is also an invitation to share multiple cultural contexts. All such invitations help to nurture a learning space that communicates 'togetherness', which is itself a key purpose of GCE work.

We recommend that you begin this lesson on 'Home Is Where Our Hearts Are' by acknowledging that there could be sensitivities around the subject. When discussing 'home' and 'homelessness', you might invite the group to ask any questions about the lesson in advance of its practice. In this way, you are giving the learners every opportunity to be mentally and emotionally prepared;

to express their feelings about issues they may rather not discuss. In our experience, having an honest conversation about so-called 'sensitive' topics with the group is the best approach. We have found that students are open to these discussions, even those who have experienced being forced to leave home or those who are still experiencing homelessness – provided, of course, that discussions are conducted in a respectful and safe environment and that the students themselves do not feel pressured to share their personal stories. It really is about being transparent and flexible about what and how much is discussed and being fair and inclusive throughout.

Activities

Learners reflect on how behaviours or actions can determine whether a person feels welcome or unwelcome, or feels like they belong or do not belong. You can develop this discussion by considering how a sense of 'not belonging' can negatively impact a person's well-being. This also presents a hopeful opportunity to consider how to create a sense of belonging; how to make someone else feel like they belong. Again, this is an important prelude to lessons which follow on migration, especially when we consider how a person seeking asylum may feel isolated, lost and/or like they do not belong. In engaging in this foundational lesson, learners may develop a deeper empathy for refugees and asylum seekers in their local community who may feel (or who may be made to feel) like they are not part of the community. This lesson helps students to think more critically about what causes asylum seekers and refugees to feel such isolation and to question systemic practices which purposefully separate them from the rest of the community (such as the system of Direct Provision). Most importantly, students and teachers have an opportunity to come together and take some action (however small). In this lesson, you can consider creative ways to develop supports for Others to nurture their sense of belonging. In later lessons, you can explore how to implement these ideas in your own lives and in local communities.

The 'Home' activity enables learners to consider the value of home; how people can feel safe and comforted by things they have in their homes. Students will indicate, for example, particular smells or furniture pieces; how objects at home remind them of their loved ones; home items and local places that are meaningful to them, that provide them with a strong sense of belonging. You could invite the learners to present their collages on 'home' to the rest of the group. This is an important lesson to do before exploring 'homelessness' as it helps learners understand how much more a person can lose other than the physical space of a house. However, care must be taken with the subject. We all come to understand that the basic provision of shelter is something that we all need, but we also get a deeper sense of home, belonging, and identity – 'things' we need in order to flourish. Throughout this lesson, learners are invited to imagine all the things they love about home. They are also invited – in a critically unsettling (but safe) manner – to consider what it might be like to leave home unexpectedly.

In the second activity, students are invited to create a bridge that holds as many paper cups on it as possible. The bridge must be at least 20 cm above a surface. It must be self-supporting, using only the materials that are provided. At the end of the task, the bridge must remain standing. Use your own judgement to see how long the students should be given to complete the task, but we suggest 30 to 40 minutes for the entire activity. The objective of using the grapes is to represent the unpredictable problems that can cause pressure at home; problems like illness, unemployment, rent increases that cause instability at home and even force people into homelessness. It is important for young people to have space to discuss whether everyone has a right to have a safe and secure place to call home. Perhaps students may make wider links – for example, that having a safe and secure place to call 'home' enables people to contribute positively to their local community and wider society?

Homelessness is a very real issue in local and global contexts and therefore, in the words of Paulo Freire, this offers us a 'teachable moment'. Try not to feel intimidated by the reality of this topic. There is a stigma attached to homelessness that is unhelpful when learning about social and political injustices. Exploring the issue with honesty, integrity and sensitivity has much more potential for developing critical awareness amongst our students and, simultaneously, giving democratic value to what young people think and have to say. There may indeed be learners (students and teachers) who have experienced homelessness – such is the reality of today's world – so signalling learners' rights to share or not share in this discussion is (as mentioned) important.

Table 4.1 shares some facts about homelessness, adapted from the websites of Crisis UK (2019) and Homelessness Ireland, which you can share with the other learners in your group. The information in the table also could be used to inspire ideas for taking action – such as raising awareness by sleeping outside for a night with your class; campaigning in the school and local community; writing to local politicians and government to take action against homelessness, etc. Students come to learn that unexpected events in a person's life can place enormous strain that may lead to homelessness, such as: relationship breakdowns; losing a job; mental or physical health problems; or substance misuse.

In our experience, this lesson on 'home' is incredibly helpful in building empathy. It can enable young people to move away from 'labelling and blaming' to explore multiple reasons why people can be driven into homelessness. In the GCE classroom, the objective is to "improve hearts and minds" and to nurture political awareness and change (Hess & McAvoy, 2014, p.16).

Reflection

You might recall from **Lesson 1** how we expressed the importance of critically exploring "how global justice issues interlink with their everyday lives" and how "informed and engaged citizens are best placed to address complex social, economic and environmental issues linked to development" (Irish Aid, 2017, p.6). Approaching issues such as homelessness and examining the root causes of local and global homelessness with young people, provides crucial learning. It validates their curiosity, and (possible) experiences, by creating an honest platform for discussion on very real world issues that concern them either directly or indirectly. It is helpful for the teacher to reflect on: Why you have decided to engage in this type of teaching and learning?; what is it that you hope to achieve?; and what are your own values that have brought you here? Reflecting on our own values and desires for a better way to live together can naturally open the door to *your* political classroom (Hess & McAvoy, 2014).

Table 4.1: Homelessness Facts

Homelessness is devastating, dangerous and isolating.

The average age of death for people experiencing homelessness is 46 for men and 42 for women.

People sleeping on the street are almost 17 times more likely to have been victims of violence.

More than one in three people sleeping rough have been deliberately hit or kicked or experienced some other form of violence whilst homeless.

Homeless people are over nine times more likely to take their own life than the general population.

Finland has all but eradicated rough sleeping and housed a significant number of long-term homeless people, so it is possible to end homelessness.

In Ireland: According to figures published by the Department of Housing, Local Government & Heritage, the number of people accessing State-funded emergency accommodation as of March 2024 is 13,866. There are a total of 20,001 people living in Direct Provision and emergency international protection accommodation, according to the Department of Integration (Fletcher, 2023).

In the UK: There is no national figure for how many people are homeless across the UK. This is because homelessness is recorded differently in each nation, not accurately recorded or not recorded at all. Estimates include more than 200,000 households in England alone. Known as core homelessness, it includes rough sleeping, people living in sheds, garages and other unconventional buildings, sofa surfing, hostels and unsuitable temporary accommodation such as B&Bs or Refugee Centres.

Causes	Types	Take Action
Lack of affordable housing. Poverty. Unemployment. Life events that push people into homelessness: • Leaving the prison system; • Leaving the care system; • Discharged from the army with no home to go to; • Escaping a violent or abusive relationship; • Can no longer afford the rent.	**Rough sleeping:** The most visible form and often combined with challenges around trauma, mental health and drug misuse. **Statutory homelessness:** Every year, tens of thousands of people apply to their local authority for homelessness assistance. **Hidden homelessness:** Many people who are not entitled to help with housing stay in hostels, squats or B&Bs, in overcrowded accommodation or 'concealed' housing, such as the floors or sofas of friends and family. **At risk of homelessness:** Some people are more at risk of being pushed into homelessness than others; people in low paid jobs, living in poverty and poor quality or insecure housing are more likely to experience homelessness.	**Donate** **Volunteer** **Campaign** **Raise awareness**

Source: Crisis UK (2019) and Homelessness Ireland.

Lesson Plan 4: Home is Where Our Hearts Are

Purpose of this lesson (learning objectives):
- To share ideas and vocabulary around the concept of belonging;
- To develop our understanding of the pressure which can lead to homelessness;
- To build empathy for people who are without homes (locally and globally);
- To acknowledge the resilience required to build a new home.

Teacher Materials:
- String
- Newspapers/magazines (or Google images and Google slides)
- A ream of paper
- Paper clips
- Grapes
- Sticky tape
- Paper cups (collect used coffee cups from pupils/staff)
- Marker pens
- Space (consideration to seating and space for movement and somewhere you don't mind getting wet and messy)

Format:
Flexible group learning

	Activity	Let's talk about it
Lead in 'Home'	Write the word 'Home' on the board or on a large sheet. Explain that we want to explore the notion of 'home'. Encourage creative thinking and ask if it is just a physical place, or if 'home' means more than that? Ask the students, working individually at first, to reflect and record their ideas on Post-its. Invite creative responses: they can use single words, a sentence, an image, symbol, line from a song. They might mention objects, memories, an emotion, a taste, smell or sound… Everyone will have their own ideas and perception of Home, and their own way of conveying it. Form small groups to share and discuss ideas (as they feel comfortable). Write each word on a Post-it and then place it on the board. Then collect the Post-its and read them out as you place their ideas around the word 'Home'. Invite observations from the whole group.	Today, we are going to explore the concept of 'Home' and how it relates to identity and a sense of belonging. When you think of home, what words come to mind? How can the question "Where do you come from?" create a sense of 'belonging' or 'not belonging'?

	Activity	Let's talk about it
'Belonging'/'Not Belonging'	On a wall, place the words 'Belonging' and 'Not Belonging' at either end of the line, connected by string. Individually, students write words about belonging or not belonging on the sticky notes provided – each idea on a separate sticky note – and place them on the wall line. Positioning them along the line, according to whether they strongly influence a sense of belonging/not belonging.	I would like to invite you to think along with me, about the meaning of both Belonging and Not Belonging. What words do we associate with Belonging? For example, 'connection'. What words do we associate with Not Belonging? For example, 'isolation'. Can you think of things you could do (actions, responses, support etc.) to turn some of those 'Not Belonging' feelings into a greater sense of connection, and move them further up the line? What might a person in a new place feel? How might their feelings range? What might influence a person's capacity to deal with new situations? Can you think of ways you could personally help someone to feel closer to 'Belonging'? Are there any 'big ideas' that could help people to feel connected, and do we have power to help make those changes happen?
Making a collage	Ask students to find images and words they associate with home and make a collage. (This activity can be done using magazines and newspapers or digitally using images and the snipping tool.) Invite students to walk around the room and look at each other's collages (alternatively you could ask students to present their collages).	Are there any common elements, symbols, or concepts that emerge? Are there any that particularly resonate with you? Can you see connections between the objects you chose and your understanding of home, or belonging?

	Activity	**Let's talk about it**
Building bridges	Divide your groups into teams of at least three. Distribute the materials evenly between the groups. Ensure everyone in each group has a cup. Ask your group to think of the cup as their home. Using a marker, ask your group to call out something that is important to them at home and why. If it's important to them and others, ask them to draw a line on the cup to indicate how important it is to them. For example, If they say "food" and others agree that it is important to them too, then everyone draws a line a quarter of the way up from the bottom of the cup with "food" written next to it. Once everyone has thought of all the things that might be important, and everybody's cup has a few things written on it, ask the group to put their cups aside. The next step is to build a bridge that holds as many paper cups on it as possible. The bridge must be at least 20cm above a surface. It must be self-supporting using only the materials provided (a ream of paper, paper clips, sticky tape). At the end of the task, the bridge must remain standing. Give the group as long as you think necessary to complete this task. Explain that their bridges represent the group and their homes. Their cups will be filled to the top line to indicate what would happen if a sudden pressure such as illness, someone at home losing a job, families separating could do to their "home bridge". Once the cups are filled with sweets/grapes, ask the groups to carefully place their cups on their bridge where they feel it will be supported. The bridges may hold or collapse. Ask the group what materials they would have liked to help strengthen their bridge and prevent it from falling or coping with the extra pressure of the filled cups.	Some of your bridges would have been weaker or stronger depending on how you built it. What do you think the bridge exercise tells us about homelessness? Identify points where you think people sit at the brink of homelessness – just before the pressure is too much, and the bridge breaks. Most of us have our family or friends for support if we were ill or had nowhere to live. So not everyone is at risk of homelessness. How did it make you feel to know that some people don't have support when the pressure of something unexpected happens? Most people can cope with one or two unexpected pressures but, when pressure is constant, it can build up and push someone into homelessness. Can you think what these pressures might be? Do you think homelessness can be prevented? If yes, how? If no, why not? What practical things do you think should be put in place to prevent homelessness? (This could be as simple as speaking to someone about their housing needs before they leave care or a hospital, or larger initiatives such as building a set number of affordable homes a year).

	Activity	Let's talk about it
Video: Hiba's Story	Show the video: *Hiba's Story* (https://youtu.be/7QVmXX62_H0, YouTube video, '*Hiba's Story: Ten-Year-Old Syrian Refugee* UNICEF USA [3.03 minutes]).	What is happening in this short film extract? How do you feel watching it? What are the challenges faced by Hiba and her family? How might these challenges have affected her? What part of the film do you find most memorable? What would you like to ask Hiba?
Get creative	Give students the instructions for making their own 'zine (**Worksheet 4.1**). Students consider all their learning regarding the theme of home and homelessness, but locally and globally, and create their own little books.	You are going to create 'zines (little books) which tell a story about home and homelessness.
Make a movie	Show students the trailer for the graphic novel *Illegal* (https://youtu.be/cnWeuPNl5dY, YouTube video, *Illegal* by Eoin Colfer & Andrew Donkin, Book Trailer, Sourcebookinc [1.08 minutes]).	What do we see? What do we hear? How does the trailer communicate a message of home or homelessness? Students use phone movie app to create their own movies that communicate an understanding about home/homelessness locally and/or globally (https://www.makeuseof.com/how-to-create-movie-trailers-on-iphone/)

Time to think
How has your understanding of the idea of movement and forced migration changed? How might it feel to have barriers which prevent you from following your dreams? How might you feel if you were to arrive somewhere new? How might you use this knowledge and understanding to welcome refugees to your community? What simple acts could you carry out in order to show support for refugees in your local community?

These lessons are adapted from:
Beyond Borders (Vicky Donnelly): https://galwayowc.wordpress.com/beyond-borders/
Crisis UK: https://www.crisis.org.uk/get-involved/resources-for-young-people/
Building Bridges: https://www.scouts.org.uk/activities/a-safe-bridge/.

Worksheet 4.1: Making a 'zine

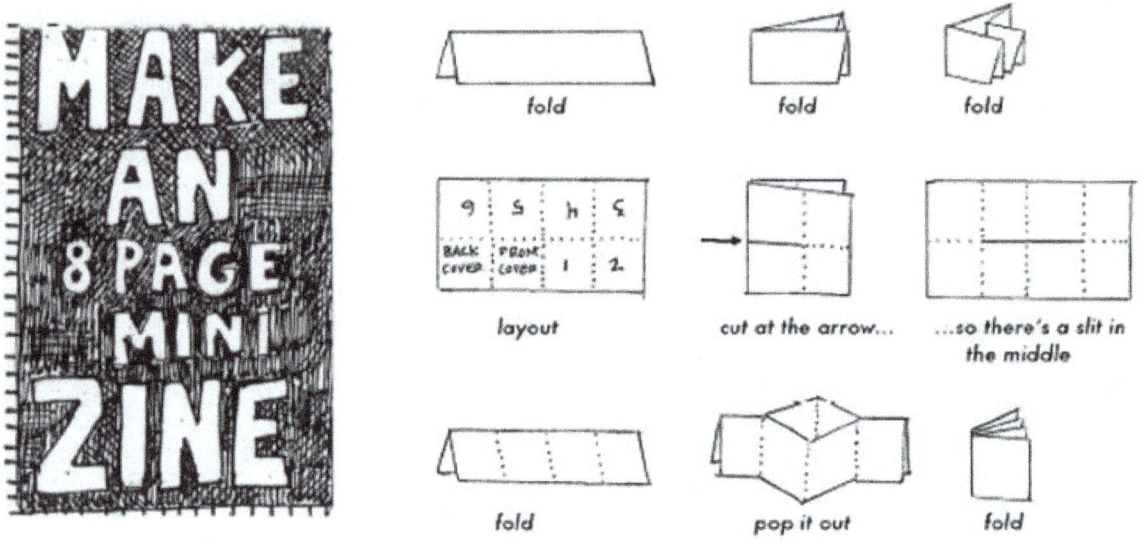

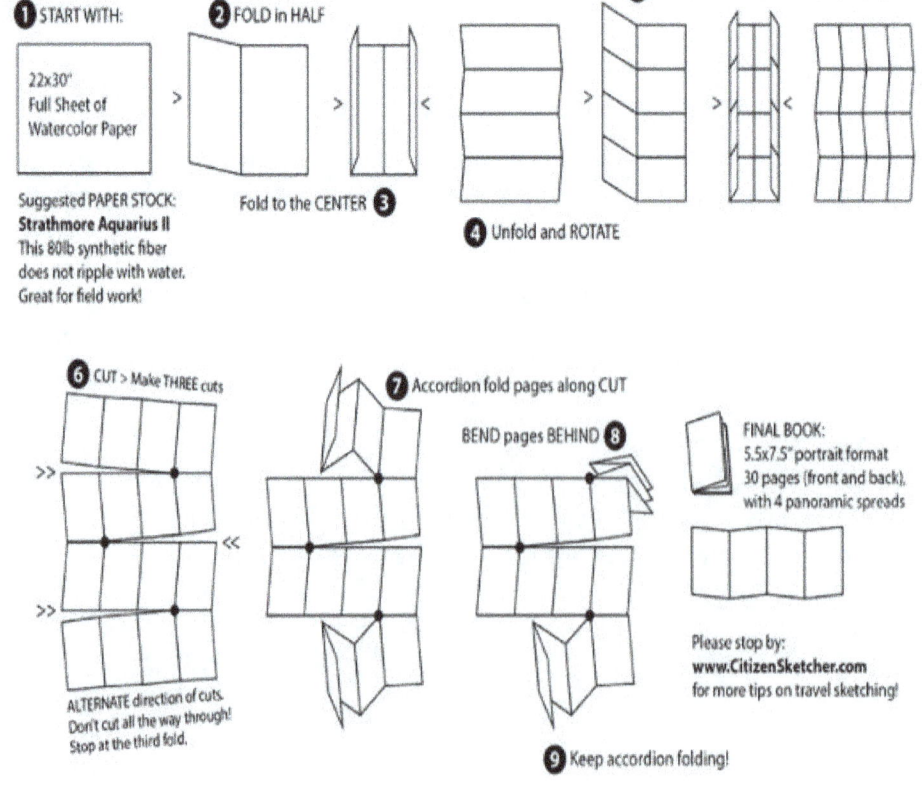

Reproduced by kind permission of Elize de Beer, Printmaker/Artist/Sculptor, Cork (www.elizedebeer.com)

LESSON 5: OUR MULTIPLE IDENTITIES

Appreciation of difference and multiple identities and the development of skills for living in a progressively more diverse world are key aims of Global Citizenship Education (UNESCO, 2015). UNESCO suggests that multiple identities include recognising culture, language, religion, gender, and our common humanity. Through learning about their own multiple identities, students may come to understand their global citizenship character, including an appreciation of diversity and a respect for difference:

Learners learn about their identities and how they are situated within multiple relationships (for example, family, friends, school, local community, country), as a basis for understanding the global dimension of citizenship. They develop an understanding of difference and diversity (for example, culture, language, gender, sexuality, religion), of how beliefs and values influence people's views about those who are different, and of the reasons for and impact of, inequality and discrimination. Learners also consider common factors that transcend difference, and develop the knowledge, skills, values and attitudes required for respecting difference and living with others. (UNESCO, 2015, pp.23-24).

This *Handbook* is concerned with GCE for students at upper secondary level, for which the learning objective outlined by UNESCO is that students will be able to "critically examine ways in which different levels of identity interact and live peacefully with different social groups" (UNESCO, 2015, p.35).

Guidance

Traditionally, citizenship education was focused on promoting the nation state and tended to sideline any deviation from a singular and patriotic version of citizenship. This view relegated those parts of peoples' identities that did not fit in with this (nationalised) vision of citizenry. Consequently, alternative cultures were less valued as they were generally not considered to be representative of (that) society. Thus, many people were (often, implicitly) taught that their identity was peripheral. This narrow vision of citizenship (and the ways in which to educate about citizenship) has now changed in Ireland and in many other progressive countries. Banks (2008) rejects the narrow purpose of citizenship to assimilate different people to a generic national identity as inadequate because the world is becoming increasingly diversified and marginalised groups are (quite rightly) seeking cultural recognition. Accordingly, an education that emphasises multicultural citizenship is being promoted, whereby students learn not just about the nation-state to which they 'belong' (as legal citizens), but also about their own cultural heritages and global-local communities (to which they also 'belong'). By looking at such complex identities and seeing how they inter-relate with people 'everywhere', we, as teachers, can help raise awareness and generate action on issues of global concern – not least in relation to the big global issues of our time, such as global warming, war, migration and epidemics. The importance of these global links between people is also noted by Gundara (2008), who calls for active citizenship tasks to 're-connect' with isolated individuals, groups and communities in diverse societies in order to 'bowl together'. This sporting analogy emphasises the strength of 'the team over the individual' and helps students to understand the need for collective effort for collective success.

Pashby (2018, p.283) helpfully identifies three considerations when engaging with discussions on citizenship and identity:

- Need for a flexible conception of citizenship that includes multiple and overlapping identities;
- Recognition and addressing of the roots of social exclusion inherent in the concept of citizenship itself;
- Promotion of a complex sense of common humanity and solidarity across difference.

Further, Bellucci-Buckelew & Fishman (2011) outline two different identity lists – the A list and the B list (**Table 5.1**). The A list refers to race, ethnicity, religion, gender and nationality – identities often associated with the term multiculturalism. In addition, they can be used in combinations with each other – for example, Irish-Catholic or Black-American-woman. They can also be used in combinations with B list features, which includes class, age, geography, education, occupation, family status and sexual orientation. Thus one can be Irish-Catholic-educated-working class or a Black-American-woman-single-parent. A list combination (both within and across lists) often can be the source of unflattering and enduring stereotypes.

Table 5.1: A and B lists (per Bellucci-Buckelew & Fishman)

'A' List Characteristics	'B' List Characteristics
Race	Class
Ethnicity	Age
Religion	Geography
Gender	Education
Nationality	Occupation
	Family status
	Sexual orientation

Bellucci-Buckelew & Fishman (2011) point out that A list identities on their own are inadequate and miss the complexity of the factors that are involved in the creation of everyone's identity. They note that people who have more in common with the dominant identity often feel that multiculturalism is only relevant to 'them' (people of other ethnicities) rather than 'us'. Interestingly, dominant groups in society can assume individual or group identities, while subordinated groups are generally assigned a single identity – most often, associated with their ethnicity (Gundara, 2010). Gundara also warns that the prevalence of racism and a dearth of democratic engagement are key factors in explaining why dominant groups present as a singular identity (often based on nationality), while minority groups respond to this in ways that (re)-emphasise a singular identity (often based on religion). To overcome emphases on singular identity, Bellucci-Buckelew & Fishman (2011) advocate a combination of A and B list identities to offset negative stereotypes and to provide a positive personal understanding of, and association with, multiculturalism for *all* students. People who seem almost identical in terms of the A list see their identities and their relationships enhanced by adding the B list descriptors. Conversely, people who appear very different in the A list can be connected in unforeseen ways when the B list is included.

Activities

In **Lesson 2**, you explored the question of identity. The purpose of the introductory exercise in this lesson is to examine our 'multiple identities'. You might begin the lesson by explaining to students how identity is important to defining 'who we are and how others see us'. This brainstorming exercise should identify the different range of factors that the students associate with 'identity'. Ask what areas of a person's identity we associate with 'multiculturalism' – you will probably find very broad features/characteristics that note ethnicity, religion and/or race.

You might then ask students to individually write the words they would use to describe their identities on **Worksheet 5.1**. As this is an area that some students may feel uncomfortable with, we suggest that you explain that this is a personal exercise – that responses will not be revealed to the class unless students wish to share them. Ask the students to consider their cultural, national and global identities. Question which identity they most identify with. We have found that this differs depending on the students themselves and/or the classroom profile. Interestingly, transnational identities, such as EU citizenship and global identities, tend to be less prevalent. You could follow these questions by asking which aspects of a person's identity set them apart from the different groups to which they belong. As this area has the potential to raise some sensitive issues, we advise you to preface your questions with a reminder to students of the need to be respectful in their responses.

Then ask the students to work together in groups on **Worksheet 5.2**. Initially, students are tasked with categorising the words as A or B list words. You should explain that the A list refers to the most 'identifiable' aspects of one's identity. Question why each characteristic is considered an aspect of a person's identity. A way of highlighting the dominance of the A list is to ask the students how they would describe someone famous, such as a named actor, sports star or singer. As this list contains some of the most commonly-held beliefs around identity, it is likely that many of the responses will come from the A list. Ask the students to identify other aspects not mentioned in the lists that they would use to construct a person's identity. We have found additional student responses to include features of being: sporty; studious; funny; a Goth or 'emo'. Question whether a person can belong to many different cultures, for example. This is useful for pointing out that we all have different cultures and it especially reminds us that multiculturalism is about 'us' and not simply about 'others'. You could point out that some people may feel that certain aspects pertaining to religion or sexual orientation, for example, relate to *personal* identity, whereas others may consciously wear garments or objects to display their *religious* identity. Question the students on why people may not want to include all aspects of their identities, and ask them why people may wish to appear similar to others.

The next exercise examines how people may appear to be culturally very different on an external level, yet may share many similarities on a deeper level. The extract on **Worksheet 5.3** is taken from Dalal Sayed's (2022) book, *Escape from War to Live in Peace*, which describes her journey from Syria to become an asylum seeker in Ireland. The excerpt recounts an event from Dalal's early days in Ireland. The aims of this exercise are to show, firstly, that leaving Syria was not something Dalal wanted to do but was forced to do because of the war and, secondly, that differences in identity are impactful, though common ground can be found by looking for similarities. The questions show how Dalal initially was viewed by others only as a Syrian refugee. The extract doesn't mention physical differences, but the photo of Dalal shows that she wears a hijab.

You could probe students as to why she may initially have been viewed as different. Question too what her A list identities are and how they may lead to stereotyped views of her. Then identify B list characteristics and question which elements were similar between Dalal and the people in Cappoquin (in Waterford, Ireland).

Emphasise that the account provided is Dalal's first-hand experience, rather than one written by a journalist based on his/her view of Dalal's identity, for example. Question students on the reasons why this primary source (or personal narrative/history) is important for learning more about Dalal's identity.

The students may already have encountered Yusra Mardini's story in the film *The Swimmers*, which will be referenced also in **Lesson 9** of the *Handbook*. The purpose of this exercise is to look at two women from different parts of the world – to examine their different cultures and who share some common identities. We suggest that you begin by asking the students to read the passages in **Worksheet 5.4**. Ask them to underline or circle any elements that refer to each woman's identities. If students know more about either woman, they may add this information. Note all the identities they identify on the whiteboard or electronic notepad.

Then ask students to work in pairs to discuss each woman's A list identities. This should show the two women as quite different, with perhaps only one obvious common identity – gender. Question whether a person's A list identity can change (*Note:* Some elements can; a person may change religion, for instance). Focus on why these identities are viewed as A list identities (you may note that these are often perceived as physically evident). Ask students to explain what this tells us about 'stereotyping'.

We suggest that you remain sensitive to your classroom profile and seek to manage discussions to prevent the students from perpetuating stereotypes. You may choose to give examples here, such as the 'drunken Irishman' (again, see **Lesson 8**) and explain how often the most hurtful stereotypes stem from people who have least contact with those people they stereotype. You could ask students for examples of stereotypical representations that they feel are not representative of them – for instance, teenagers being described as 'lazy', 'rude', 'loud', 'work-shy', etc.

Students should continue to work in pairs to identify the B list characteristics of each woman. On completion of this list, the students complete **Worksheet 5.5** (the Venn diagram). Using different colours, students can highlight areas where there is greater similarity (these most likely may emerge from the B list). It is important to stress that there are many different combinations possible in constructing people's multiple identities. This is the key learning moment in this lesson. Question whether the students share many B list factors, rather than A list factors, with their friends.

Reflection

In the reflective element of the lesson, then, it is important to reiterate how we all have multiple identities (not just one). Use questions to emphasise how people may have more in common than they have differences, and question why it is important to stress our common identities in global citizenry terms. These questions can enable us all to understand that, by finding commonalities, we are less likely to view people as 'others' – which, in turn, is premised on A list stereotypes and combinations that perpetuate 'us' and 'them' attitudes.

Ask the students to reflect on areas that they had not previously considered about identities. This will help to identify whether they have developed their thinking on multiple identities. In this lesson, much focus was given to the identities of other people – Dalal Sayed, Yusra Mardini and Simone Biles. Ask the students to revisit **Worksheet 5.1** and add any aspect of *their* own identity that they did not include initially. We suggest that students note their points in different colours to distinguish between the beginning and end of the lesson. If this is impractical, students may circle and underline their responses. Ask the students to now reconsider their own identities: what are the aspects of their personality that they would now use to identify themselves; how do they compare their original and end-of-lesson responses? If students are comfortable to talk about their value differences ('then-and-now'), allow them to share these with the class. We have found that the initial list is often quite brief and not necessarily well thought-out. Ask students whether they identified more with the A list or B list at the beginning and/or the end. This may show varied responses. We have found that the A list often features most prominently at the beginning and the B list more at the end. That said, some A list factors often remain hidden, as students take them as a 'given' – for example, one's Whiteness, Irishness, etc. A key purpose of GCE classroom work is to bring such hidden forces to light!

Lesson Plan 5: Our Multiple Identities

Purpose of this lesson (learning objectives):
To identify people's multiple identities and question stereotypes.

Teacher Materials:
- **Worksheets 5.1, 5.2, 5.3, 5.4 and 5.5**
- Pens for sharing

Format:
- Individual learning
- Paired learning

	Activity	Let's talk about it
Lead in Multiculturalism	Invite students to brainstorm the different identities people have – for example, white, Irish, Jewish, Traveller, etc. Ask students to fill out the identities they associate with themselves on **Worksheet 5.1** using a blue or black pen. Explain that they do not need to explain these to anyone else.	What areas of a person's identity do we associate with multiculturalism? Why are these considered aspects of a person's identity? Are there any other aspects that have not been mentioned? If so, what are they? Can a person belong to many different cultures? Would you include all these aspects? Why/why not?
Multiple identities	In groups, ask students to look at **Worksheet 5.2** and classify the different aspects of identity into the A List or the B List.	What aspects of a person's identity set them apart from the main groups they belong to?
Differences and similarities	Ask students, in pairs, to read the introduction to the book *Escape from War to Live in Peace* on **Worksheet 5.3** and discuss the questions.	In your opinion, what was Dalal's main identity? How do you think other people saw her? What was her view of the people she encountered?

	Activity	Let's talk about it
Shared identities	Ask students, on their own, to read the extracts on Yusra Mardini and Simone Biles in **Worksheet 5.4**, noting the main areas that they see as part of each woman's identity (using **Worksheet 5.1** as a guide). They can add other identities not listed on the worksheet. Then, in pairs, ask them to discuss each woman's A List identity: • Are they always the same? • Do you think one is prioritised over the other? • Why are they seen as each woman's main identity? Next, ask students to work alone to note the B List characteristics of each woman (using **Worksheet 5.1** as a guide). They can add other identities not listed on the worksheet. Then, in pairs, ask them to discuss each woman's B List identities: • What difference did the addition of the B List descriptors make to her identity?	Are there many shared identities between the two women? What about their differences? What do you learn from this exercise? What does this exercise tell you about stereotyping?
Venn diagram	Working in pairs, ask students to complete the Venn Diagram on **Worksheet 5.5**, noting the A List in red and the B List in blue.	If you were to add your own identities to the Venn diagram, what similarities and differences would you share with these women?
Reflection	Invite students to look again at **Worksheet 5.1** and add in any other aspects of their identity that they did not initially mention, using a red or green pen to distinguish the new aspects added to their initial answer.	

Time to think
Why is it important to be aware of the different identities that people have?

Worksheet 5.1: Describe Your Identity

Write words in the box below that you think describe your identity.
(This worksheet is for your own use and you will not need to share it with the rest of the class unless you wish to do so.)

Worksheet 5.2: A or B?

Classify the following words relating to **identity** into the A List or the B List:

    Gender
    Nationality
    Family status
    Age
    Religion
    Occupation
    Race
    Class
    Ethnicity
    Education
    Geography
    Gender
    Sexual orientation

The A List should contain the areas that are most commonly used when speaking about multiculturalism. The B List is used to show how people differ from the broad cultural groups to which they belong and are useful to prevent stereotyping.

A List Characteristics	B List Characteristics

Activity based on A-List/B-List Getting Beyond Stereotypes in Bellucci Buckelew M. & Fishman, A. (2011). *Reaching & Teaching Diverse Populations: Strategies for Moving Beyond Stereotypes.* Thousand Oaks, CA: Sage.

Worksheet 5.3: Introduction to *Escape from War to Live in Peace* by Dalal Sayed

Source: Published with permission of Waterford City & Council and Dalal Sayed.

I wrote this story so people would understand that we had homes and lives in Syria, and we didn't want to leave and come to Ireland. We had no choice.

Living here in Ireland, I saw that a few women were wary of me. I wanted to tell them: "I am a woman like you and a mother who wants a safe life for her children".

Recently, we attended a soccer match in Cappoquin. My two sons were playing with their friends. Other mothers were sitting together talking and I sat down by myself. One man came and asked me how I was. We began to talk, and he asked me about my journey here and then he called his wife and the others to come to listen. I told them about the journey that I have written about here. They said, "You are a super woman to do all that and we will read your story".

- What indicates that Dalal was not happy to leave Syria?
- Why do you think she felt that people were wary of her?
- What did she have in common with the people she met?
- Give two reasons why the man's gesture was important.
- What shared interests can you identify between these people?
- What messages does it give about different identities?
- In what ways is this account more useful than a journalist's report?

Worksheet 5.4: Yusra and Simone

Yusra Mardini

The book *Butterfly*, which was also made into a film called *The Swimmers*, tells Yusra Mardini's story.

Yusra was born on March 5, 1998, in Damascus, Syria. At a young age, Yusra and her sister Sara began swimming at a local club in Damascus and she hoped to represent Syria in the Olympic Games.

War broke out in Syria in 2011. As the violence escalated and came closer to her home, some of her friends began to leave the country in search of safety. While Yusra was training, a bomb came through the roof and landed in the pool where she was swimming, but fortunately failed to detonate. After this, Yusra and Sara decided to seek safety and refuge in Europe.

In 2015, the Mardini sisters, along with other asylum seekers, boarded an overcrowded inflatable boat to cross the Aegean Sea from Turkey to Greece. During the crossing, the motor failed, causing the boat to drop the height at which it sat over the sea, and it dipped into the water. Because it was overcrowded, it was beginning to sink. Yusra and Sara got into the water to lighten the load and swam alongside the boat. This action managed to keep the boat afloat, and they eventually reached Lesbos in Greece.

During their 25-day journey by plane, train, taxi and on foot from Greece to Germany, Yusra and her sister faced many challenges, especially leaving Hungary to get to Germany. Yusra and Sara arrived in Berlin and applied for refugee status. While in Berlin, Yusra began training again.

In 2016, Yusra made history by competing as part of the Refugee Olympic Team at the Rio de Janeiro Olympics. She also competed in Tokyo in 2021. Yusra's Olympics performances, her book and the film about her life have given her a platform to advocate for refugees.

Simone Biles

Simone Biles is the most decorated American gymnast of all time.

Simone was born on March 14, 1997, in Columbus, Ohio. When Simone was six years old, she and her sister Adria were adopted by her grandfather Ron and his wife Nellie. Her grandfather was an Air Force veteran and air traffic controller and Nellie was a nurse who owned several nursing homes in Texas.

At the age of six, while on a day trip to a gym with her childcare group, she saw girls practising gymnastics. The coaches were so impressed with Simone's efforts to copy the girls that they suggested she join the gymnastics classes.

Being a black athlete in a sport traditionally dominated by athletes of Caucasian descent, Simone's success challenged the notion that certain sports are reserved for specific racial or ethnic groups.

Simone's talent and moves, such as the "Biles", demonstrated her physical skills and her innovation within the sport. At the 2016 Olympic Games in Rio de Janeiro, Simone became only the fifth female gymnast to win four gold medals at a single Olympics.

However, the pressure of the huge expectations of her performance caused Simone to withdraw from the 2020 Tokyo Olympics (held in 2021 due to Covid-19) because of mental stress and the need to focus on her well-being. This decision led to people questioning how the pressure to succeed in sport can be very harmful to athletes' mental and emotional health. Despite this, Simone competed in the 2024 Paris Olympics, where she won three gold medals and one silver medal – making her one of the most decorated gymnasts in the history of the Olympic Games.

Person	A List Identities	B List Identities
Yusra Mardini		
Simone Biles		

Worksheet 5.5: Identity Venn Diagram

Working with your partner note in the left circle Yusra Mardini's identities and in the right circle note Simone Biles's identities.

Note the A List identities in **red** and the B List identities in **blue**.

Place the areas they have in common in the centre part of the diagram.

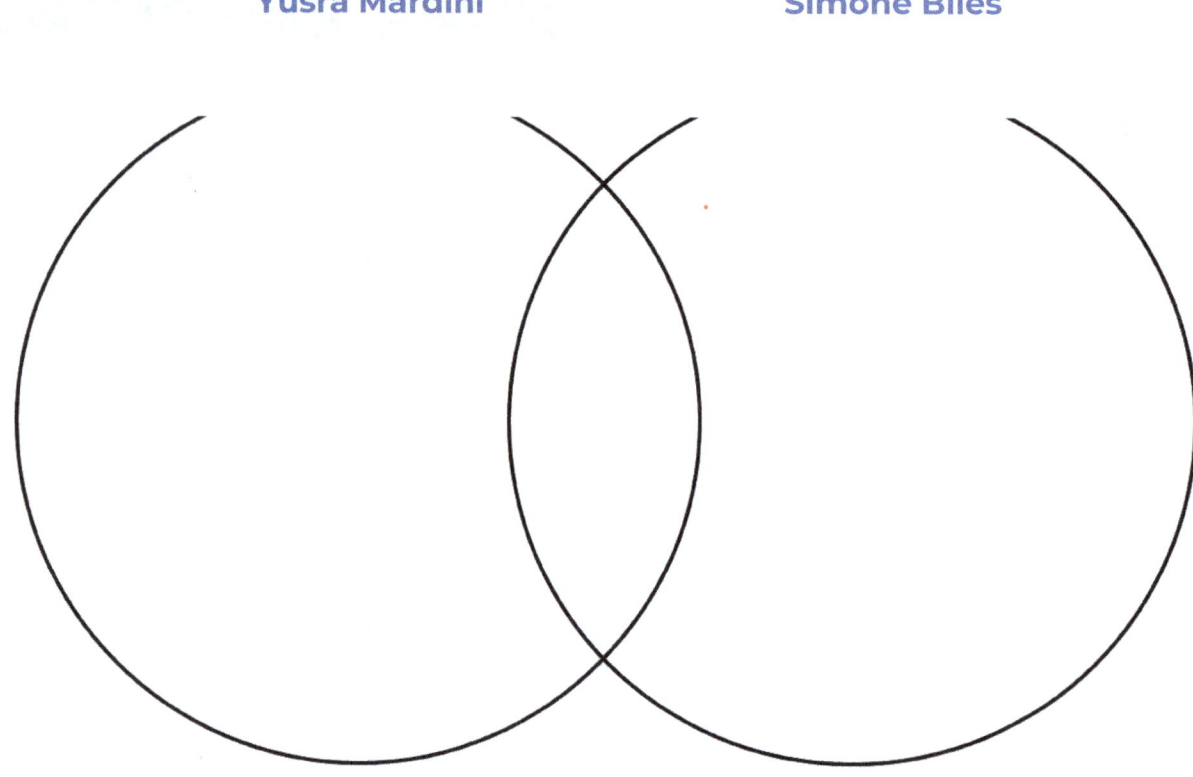

Activity based on A-List/B-List Getting Beyond Stereotypes in Bellucci Buckelew M. & Fishman, A. (2011) *Reaching & Teaching Diverse Populations: Strategies for Moving Beyond Stereotypes*. Thousand Oaks, CA: Sage.

LESSON 6:
EXPLORING STEREOTYPES

The purpose of this lesson is to explore the concept of diversity and to acknowledge, discuss and potentially debunk some of the stereotypes we make about Others, especially those from backgrounds which are different to our own. The objective is not to hide our assumptions or prejudices but to actually bring them out in the open. The GCE classroom is a space for discussion and debate. We cannot deny that, in our world, more immediately in our local communities and schools, discrimination exists and persists. We learn from collective behaviours and we learn from common-held attitudes and values. In this way, we learn both progressive and harmful values and habits from each other, though in relation to the latter, we also have the capacity to *unlearn* (Fook, 2010; Simpson, 2019). It is important to note that we make assumptions every day; that we (inadvertently or otherwise) discriminate but that we also have the capacity to change. Change often occurs organically but it can also be mediated by the GCE teacher who encourages other learners to pause, listen, think and practise inclusive, community values.

Part of learning in the GCE space is to explore our past and present and see how this shapes us and shapes our beliefs. This includes looking at the assumptions we make. In this lesson, 'Exploring Stereotypes', we are presented with a wonderful opportunity to engage in healthy debate, practise our freedom to make choices and decisions (individually and as a group) and explore our willingness to change our hearts and minds. Practising democratic skills is something which is really highlighted in this lesson as learners lead and follow, speak and listen, and, notably, agree and disagree. It is important to acknowledge that not all learners may have the same access to practising these skills. As Pierre Bourdieu (1986) highlights in his paper, 'The Forms of Capital', there is much disparity in access to various socio-cultural values, skills, knowledge and action. Differential access is often determined by privilege. In other words, some students may be well-versed in how to debate and give their evidenced opinion. Their voices have been pre-valued in multiple learning locations – home, the community and school. Look to the students in your class and notice who may be less forthcoming with their perspectives, or less able to listen to others, or who are afraid of confrontation. As teachers, we have to ask ourselves: "How can we create environments that enable *all* learners to have access to values, skills, knowledge and action?" Whilst all our students are eligible to become voting citizens, for example, some may need greater empowering opportunities for this transition to take real effect. Many factors can contribute to a reluctance to speak or share opinions, though these factors may appear 'hidden from view' – for example, factors that relate to gender inequality, racial inequality, and/or class inequality. When students themselves experience 'not being seen, heard or represented', they often can retreat into their own spaces – this may reinforce a sense of hopelessness about their power and their capacity to contribute. It is crucial to work, therefore, towards enabling students to see how powerful they can be, how valid their voices are, and how significant their vote and their presence is as active citizens in the community.

Guidance

In this lesson, the teacher is presented with an opportunity to transform traditional classroom dynamics. In **Table 6.1**, we include some ideas that the teacher can experiment with – these challenge traditional identity assumptions ('the sage on the stage'), as well as 'transmissive' approaches to teaching and learning.

Table 6.1: Challenging Identity Assumptions

Why not...

Change the physical space - use grouped tables or circle formations, or get down on the floor.

When planning, be conscious of teacher talking time – practise asking questions and getting comfortable with pauses and silences.

'Problem-pose' (to use Paulo Freire's term) and then sit among your students at their level – physically and intellectually.

Using flexible grouping, give students roles, including leadership and spokesperson roles – show learners your readiness to change power dynamics in the classroom.

Use active learning methods.

Give the students paper and pens on their tables and, if you want to use the whiteboard/ICT resource, invite the students to use it and record their contributions.

Invite all learners to move around the classroom to witness and share in others' ideas.

Pre-plan typologies of questions to encourage in-depth responses.

Be kind to yourself – GCE is a practice and a process. It takes space and time, but it is completely worth it as it has the capacity to shift practices and identities!

Before the opening activity, you might generate a whole class discussion to reach an agreement about how you should conduct yourselves as a group. **Table 6.2** offers some questions which you can pose to the group so everyone can co-create a type of 'contract' or 'charter' that will regulate your classroom work. This whole class discussion sets an important foundation for how we communicate and act in the GCE classroom.

Table 6.2: Creating a 'Classroom Charter"

The teacher could prompt students to respond to...

What should we do if we are unsure about something and have a question for the teacher?

What should we do if we are offended by something that is said?

How should we go about protecting everyone in the class from being offended?

How can we protect 'freedom of speech' but also put boundaries in place ('freedom of speech comes with responsibility')?

How can we ensure that every learner has their opportunity to speak honestly and openly?

How can we enable disagreement to occur in a respectful manner?

What should we do if someone does not honour our charter?

What kinds of actions are not in keeping with our charter?

The students are now introduced to the 'Train Journey' activity (**Worksheet 6.1**). Here, they embark on an imaginary train journey for one week. They are invited to choose three people who they would like to travel with and three with whom they would not like to travel. This activity provides an opportunity for sharing multiple and often conflicting perspectives, which is a core element of the GCE classroom. In such teaching moments, remind the students again of the importance of exercising agency and respect. You might, for instance, remind students that 'everyone is entitled to have their opinions heard' and/or 'let's try not to make any judgments about what we say' and/or 'let's ask questions rather than make judgements'. We suggest that you have already your class charter in place, so that you can refer to the agreements laid out by the students themselves. In the event of any disrespectful interactions, you may remind, 'remember what we agreed upon' and/or you may ask the student to read from the co-constructed charter.

We have provided a resource for this activity which can be adapted to suit your own classroom context, so please feel free to make any changes to the profiles of people travelling on the train. For instance, perhaps you might focus on groups who are particularly marginalised in your local community. As long as the people represent groups who are often marginalised, stereotyped and/or discriminated against, the activity will be fruitful. With this work, the students are afforded the opportunity to make choices, to justify these, to have space to disagree and, all the while, to practise 'respect', 'empathy' and communication skills. They are invited also to consider the process of group decision-making and how they have worked to resolve disagreements. The 'Train Journey' exercise enables young people to communicate honestly and practise a degree of diplomacy.

In addition to the exercise on stereotypes, you could explore the nine grounds for discrimination in Ireland (see **Table 6.3**). You can begin by asking the students to try and name the nine grounds and to consider groups who are often stereotyped and how this impacts them (begin with them, as teenagers are often stereotyped!). The table offers some ideas for discussion.

Table 6.3: Discrimination

Ways in which people are discriminated	Groups who are often discriminated against or marginalised	The impact	Discriminative phrases
Membership of the Travelling Community	The Travelling community	Higher rates of early school leaving	"Travellers do not want to go to school and learn." "They don't expect much from education."
Age	Teenagers	Poor mental and physical health	"Teenagers are moody and lazy." "Up to no good."
Family Status	Single parent Stay-at-home mother	Isolation Unequal distribution of care	"They just want to stay on social welfare."
Civil Status	Single/unmarried	Single shaming Target of intrusive questions and Government benefits for only married people	"They'll find someone to marry one day."
Disability status	People with physical and intellectual disabilities	Judgement about capability	"You don't look disabled."
Sexuality	Queer and religious groups	Mental health Struggles for fear of going against faith	"You don't look gay." "God does not approve."
Religion	Muslim women	Inhibited by external Islamophobia and male-dominated interpretations of Islam from within Muslim communities	"They don't have a voice of their own." "Muslim women are passive and uninformed about the world."
Gender	Working class women Marginalised sexual identities	Binary assumptions and ignoring fluidity of gender is oppressive to everyone	"I'm not saying 'they' for an individual person. That's just poor grammar." "There are just two pronouns: she and he."
Nationality	Irish people	Excludes the very varied population of Ireland and perpetuates the misinformed idea that we have to look like a nationality	"But where are you originally from?" "Irish people are all redheads." "Irish people drink and fight."

Ways in which people are discriminated	Groups who are often discriminated against or marginalised	The impact	Discriminative phrases
Anti-migrant racism (xenophobia)	Migrants	Votes against moves to enhance rescue provisions, increasing the number of deaths of asylum seekers/ violent protests/ community unrest	"They come here and take all our housing and our jobs."

Source: https://www.employment-matters.ie/9-grounds-discrimination/.

There are opportunities here to discuss both 'race' and 'racism'. Audrey Bryan (2012) highlights how often race and racism are misrepresented in formal curricula. The GCE classroom provides a much-needed space to have conversations with students about 'race' and 'racism' – a space that challenges 'colour blind' ideology. For instance, you could explore (in a foundational way) how race was a term that was invented to perpetuate colonialist practices. In her publication, entitled *You've Got to Teach People that Racism is Wrong and then They Won't Be Racist: Curricular Representations and Young People's Understandings of 'Race' and 'Racism'*, Bryan explains how:

> **'Race' is a social-historical construct which was used to justify imperialistic regimes and practices, and to enable the exploitation and subordination of blacks by whites.** (Bryan, 2012, p.600)

It is important to look at the history of 'race' to (re-)discover causal explanations (a key tenet of the scholarly purpose of GCE) for how we understand the term 'now'. GCE students are offered the opportunity to question our pre-assumptions about 'race' (for example, that race is concerned with biological or genetic differences) and, crucially, challenge/discredit these (McGuirk, 2023). Certain world events ('still in the making') enable the perpetuation of the notion of white race superiority and GCE students *necessarily* engage with these to understand 'race' and 'racism' more critically. The GCE teacher too – alongside other learners – may need to inter-connect lessons from Christian missionary work in the 16th century to the Trans-Atlantic slave trade system to the re-claiming of the 'Black Lives Matter' movement.

'Digging deep' to the roots of injustice is crucial in the GCE classroom. There are many ways to do this and it does not mean that you have to have knowledge expertise. One suggestion is to invite the students to do some research on what 'race' means – they might begin by investigating when the term first started to be used and why. Guide their research with structured questions that help them to critically think about 'race' and 'racism' and also invite them to examine how these play out in today's world (in both local and global ways).

More immediately, you could work together (act in solidarity) to promote antiracist perspectives in your school community. One approach is to explore how the class might become 'an ally against racism'. Taking action to develop critical awareness and solidarity is a key tenet of GCE work. To this effect, this website is a helpful resource: https://www.immigrantcouncil.ie/campaign/be-ally-against-racism.

Here, you will find clear steps on how to work together against racism. These include supportive guidance for individuals who experience racism, including:

- Assessing the safety of the situation;
- Taking action and staying with the person(s) affected.
- Showing solidarity and staying with the person(s) affected for as long as they need;
- Supporting the person(s) affected to report the incident and/or report it yourself;
- Contacting relevant authorities or An Garda Síochána immediately if the racist abuse is criminal in nature.

Positive action can always be taken together to combat racism. As a leader in your learning community, perhaps you can initiate a solidarity campaign?

Reflection

Essentially, this work aims to develop students' democratic literacy and enhance their confidence as active citizens in their local, national and global communities. The development of the value of 'empathy' in the GCE classroom is crucial and this certainly surfaces when we invite students to reflect on how the excluded people (those who they have *not* chosen for their train journey) might feel.

In such ways, the 'affective' dimension of learning emerges in the GCE classroom. Specific values are nurtured in the praxis classroom: material values but also (and very importantly) affective values. The cultivation of specific *affective* values is central to a praxiological approach. The praxiological teacher works on building those values: within themselves; within the curriculum; and between learners who are committed to challenging oppressive systems and societies. Nurturing democratic values, such as equality, freedom and justice, aids the students' critical awareness that learning is truly lifelong. You, the teacher, are also invited to learn alongside the students throughout your own lifelong journey. We have seen that regular practice of exercises such as these, enable us all to feel more confident as active citizens, more capable of making our political voices heard and more aware about the possibility of change. In time, we hope that you will find that the learning community (more immediately, *your* GCE class) becomes a place of mutual responsibility and shared values and experiences. Core GCE *values* – which are nurtured over time – help learners in their understanding of *who* they are in relation to the world and *why*.

Lesson Plan 6: Exploring Stereotypes

Purpose of this lesson (learning objectives):
- To explore diversity;
- To discuss the assumptions and stereotypes we make about others;
- To reflect on how prejudices can lead to discrimination and then to exclusion.

Teacher Materials:
- Whiteboard
- Paper and pens

Format:
- Individual learning
- Small group learning

	Activity	Let's talk about it
Lead in Train Journey activity	Invite students to go on a hypothetical train journey, the duration of which will be one week. Share the list of people (see **Worksheet 6.1**) and explain that individually the students must choose three people from the list to travel in the train compartment with them (three people with whom they want the most to spend time) and choose three people with whom they do not want to travel. They have only 10 minutes to decide about the six people. Then, they must explain their choices to the others in their group. Finally, as a group (maximum four people), they must reach a consensus about your six train companions.	How did you decide and why did you choose to travel with these people? How did you decide and why did you choose to not travel with these people? During this activity, what stereotypes were revealed? (Consider: people, group and/or behaviour stereotypes). How do you think those who were eliminated/not chosen would feel and react to your choices?
Racism	Ask students what they understand by 'racism'. Then ask if they can name the nine grounds for discrimination in Ireland – share **Table 6.3** with them, as needed. Next, start a group discussion on groups who are discriminated against and how it might affect them.	

Time to think
What do you think was the purpose of this activity? What did you come to realise or learn by participating in this activity? Were you surprised by anything?

Worksheet 6.1: The Train Journey

Your potential train journey companions:

A Brazilian sex-worker	A Palestinian activist	A Trump supporter
A single mother	A British vandal	A police officer
A French farmer, who speaks only French	A drunk Russian skinhead	A GAA player from Cork
A fat Swiss banker	A beggar	A gender-diverse feminist
A newly-wedded bride	A blind Austrian accordionist	A young artist with AIDS
An Irish author	A Bosnian ex-prisoner	An American lawyer

Choose **six** people from the grid above – three to travel with you; three not to travel with you.

Explain why you chose them – and why you rejected the others.

Activity inspired by Curriculum & Development Unit (2017). *The Dice Project – A Teacher's Handbook: Journeys Exploring Migration and Migrant Rights in the Primary Classroom*, p.21

LESSON 7:
MORAL DILEMMAS

Moral education is concerned with developing global citizens who are ready to inform themselves about key global issues and challenge issues, such as combatting climate change, nurturing peaceful co-existence and developing an economic growth model that positively impacts everyone on the planet (Huo *et al.*, 2023). Acquiring and practising a sense of morality remains integral to Global Citizenship Education.

Misco (2018) outlines five key considerations for morality from a GCE perspective:

- The more viewpoints students are exposed to the better their capacity to place themselves 'in the place of others' and the more valid their final conclusions;
- Both local and global universal obligations can and do co-exist and providing a framework to negotiate conflicts between them is a central purpose of a global morality;
- Being open-minded and accepting of one's fallibility is key and being aware of its likelihood to change is important;
- Moral issues requiring immediate public attention tend to be controversial. While teachers are reluctant to engage in such issues, their discussion helps students understand how the world systems work and how the effects of change can help or hurt others. Engaging students in (so-called) 'controversial issues' allows them to develop as agents of change;
- All ideas and conclusions should be held tentatively and must assume a falsifiability.

Moral education is largely viewed within the remit of 'extra-curricular' activities rather than in classroom activities (Schuitema *et al.*, 2008). When moral education is included in curricula, it has two principal objectives – the personal development and welfare of students and the benefits of moral education for society (Schuitema *et al.*, 2008). Thus, it may be (erroneously) viewed in marginalised terms; as something separate from the curriculum, associated with so-called 'non-academic' subjects. The former objective sees moral education located in subjects that are aimed at promoting personal and social education amongst student cohorts. The latter objective is most frequently associated with citizenship or democratic education. While citizenship education has many benefits (John & Morris, 2004; Whiteley, 2014), it too is often seen as peripheral to the curriculum (O'Brien, 2023a) and its provision can differ depending on school gender profiles (O'Brien, 2023b; Tormey & Gleeson, 2012) and on students' differential socio-economic status (O'Brien, 2023c; Wood, 2014). Many moral education programmes promote a Problem-Based Learning (PBL) approach to instruction, using co-operative culture and critical discussions to develop communication, to encourage students to resolve differences of opinion and to tolerate disagreement (Schuitema et al., 2008). Some commonly-used teaching methods for promoting moral development include the use of the creative arts like drama and literature, as well as the work of activists and those involved in so-called 'service-learning'.

Guidance

Using moral dilemmas in education makes it possible for students to examine values from differing viewpoints (Veugelers, 1997). In considering the perspectives of others, moral dilemmas aim to promote tolerance, respect and open-mindedness (Schuitema et al., 2008). Kvalnes (2019, p.12) describes a dilemma as "a situation requiring a choice between two options that are, or seem to be, equally undesirable or unsatisfactory". There may be no moral element to dilemmas, such as choosing between purchasing two items such as a shirt and a book. In a *moral* dilemma, "the decision maker has to prioritise one moral value over another... it is impossible to live up to one's moral conviction and beliefs regarding how one should behave in that situation" (Kvalnes, 2019, p.12). Moreover, not all moral dilemmas are equally balanced, meaning that, in all cases, something of moral value may be lost when a decision is made. In some cases, of course, it may not be difficult to make a moral decision. The moral dilemmas, such as those included in this lesson, deal with exaggerated impersonal scenarios. This allows the discussion to take place without personalising it. That said, as Huo et al. (2023) found, teachers prefer to use real-life scenarios as they appear more attractive and meaningful and better for preparing students for life. For this reason, we suggest some additional scenarios. It is important to acknowledge that engaging in moral dilemmas does not necessarily mean that students will empathise with the people involved in the situation. At the same time, understanding how others feel and think in situations, especially where they suffer injustice, helps to nurture empathy and moral feeling (Ruiz & Vallejos, 1999). Thus, while Verducci (2000) warns against presupposing that students automatically will feel empathy when presented with stories about others or that teachers can link students' imagination to empathy, students may be prompted to develop empathy through the employment of explicit teaching methods.

Drama presents as an exemplar. Exposing students to theatre, for instance, can increase their tolerance for, and understanding of, others' emotions (Greene et al., 2018). Verducci (2000) suggests that to play a role, an actor must make the inner, emotional and psychological life of a character 'real'. Using drama alone will not cultivate empathy, but when practised following clear guidance by the teacher, students can enhance their capacity to empathise. Moreover, developing empathy through drama techniques is more effectively employed in a cross-curricular manner; 'not just in drama class'. Such a cross-curricular approach to using drama is supported by others (for example, Day, 2002) who advocate its suitability both to the formal curriculum and to GCE work. Drama holds the potential to engage moral issues in a non-threatening way because of its use of fictionalised characters and because it enables initial feelings of sympathy for characters that may translate to empathy (Day, 2002). In addition, drama can prompt a desire for action at an individual level but also, with adult guidance, a desire for collective action, such as campaigning or fundraising. We have found that the potential to develop collective action is often lost when teachers do not consider the cross-curricular potential of moral education. In addition to developing empathy, drama has the potential to allow students to overcome a lack of direct experience with the topic studied and still become engaged with and aware of real-life issues, such as uneven power dynamics in society (Saddington & McConnell, 2024). Simulation and role-playing allow students to critically synthesise information from various sources, structure debate with peers and take on the roles of representatives of/for various communities – regardless of such issues not being directly felt and/or experienced in their everyday lives.

Elliot *et al.* (2015) suggest three reasons for using drama in citizenship education:

- Citizenship education is concerned with public issues.
- Many dramas focus on social and political issues.
- Process drama may help young people think, express viewpoints, develop skills of participation and advance feelings. Specifically, drama enables young people to experience emotion in a way that allows mature responses to challenging issues.

There are several different, but essentially interchangeable, terms such as 'drama in education' and 'process drama' used to describe the process of using drama as an educational method. For consistency, we will use the term 'process drama', defined by Wells & Sandretto (2017, p.182) as:

> **A model of drama in education in which the students work within a variety of drama conventions and improvised roles alongside their teacher, who also often works in role to guide and structure the drama. The purpose of process drama is for the students to participate in learning inquiry, or discovery, rather than present a rehearsed performance to an audience.**

Teachers who employ process drama develop the capacity to nurture greater empathy in and between students. Process drama:

- Is improvised;
- Is focused on the process and not on the outcome;
- Does not emphasise the quality of the performance;
- Does not require costumes, props or accents;
- Is not performed to an external audience.

An advantage of using process drama is that students fundamentally enjoy it (Verducci, 2000). We have found that this enjoyment helps engage students in the activities and, because of the improvised nature of the task, there is no pressure to learn scripts and perform. It is also likely to encourage all class members to become involved and it promotes greater communication in the classroom.

It is important to prepare a task to be completed and to create a suitable pretext. Dunn (2016) suggests that an effective pretext:

- Raises questions for the 'reader';
- Provokes emotions and our intellect;
- Creates strong visual images;
- Has an element of ambiguity.
- Offers open-ended possibilities;
- Allows the teacher to 'see' what the students will be doing and learning in response;
- Involves a group of people;
- Indicates a future or a past;
- Offers 'a hook' for the students.

You, as the teacher, may choose to participate in role in the drama. This has advantages, including that the students can see you demonstrate what is expected, which, in turn, makes them less self-conscious and more interested in the activity. Don't worry – the teacher role may be very light, such as a TV presenter. It requires no accent, costume or props. By simply saying "Welcome to tonight's programme", the students are immediately encouraged to 'buy into' the drama. On completion of role-play activities, it is important to encourage the students to pause and reflect. While students enjoy the drama process, they frequently miss the purpose of the activity. Thus, they need guidance from the teacher to be able to reflect upon and analyse their work.

There are many different process drama techniques, such as freeze-framing, thought tracking, hot seating and simulated debate. We have chosen to use 'hot seating' in this lesson as it is a relatively straightforward process drama method. It requires no extra space or any specialist resources. In addition, it is less intimidating for students as they can play the role seated at their chairs, or someone may be designated each time to sit on a 'special chair'. This method helps the students to identify multiple perspectives as they engage with the characters expressing conflicting views of the various interested and affected parties. In hot seating, one or more students take on the role of characters associated with the given issue. They take their position in the 'hot seat', where they must answer questions put to them by the rest of the class. According to Neelands & Goode, (2015, p.43):

[Hot seating] ... highlights characters' motivations and personal dispositions; encouraging insights into relationships between attitudes and events and how events affect attitudes, encouraging reflective awareness of human behaviour.

It may be best to hot seat several characters at once. This allows you to explore a situation in detail and, because it involves more people, it is less demanding on individual students. The characters can sit at the top of the classroom facing their classmates and take questions from the other students. Students may perform as themselves or in role, but by asking them to assume the role, they may find this less uncomfortable. Invite the students themselves to make the decision to act in character or otherwise. Perhaps by taking on a different personality, they can ask questions they would not themselves ask. This itself allows them to look at the issue from a different point of view.

Activities

The purpose of the introductory exercise in this lesson is to examine what is meant by a 'moral dilemma'. You might explain to students how some decisions can be difficult because of conflicting viewpoints. Begin by asking students what their understanding of a dilemma is. Once they have completed this, ask them what they think is meant by a *moral* dilemma. Ask students to complete **Worksheet 7.1**, individually. The four scenarios contained on the worksheet are commonly used scenarios for moral reasoning. You may decide to include others that you think are more relevant to the students themselves, such as: 'You just saw your summer exam script on the teacher's desk. Do you take a photo of it or not?' or 'Your friend is telling her parents that she is going to supervised study, but instead is hanging out with older students who may be leading her into trouble. Do you tell on her?'. Having completed the worksheet individually, the students then work in pairs to discuss their responses and note the similarities and differences in their replies. Ask them to focus on the factors they considered when they made their decisions and what aspects of each decision were the most challenging.

In taking feedback from the different pairs, note first the most common responses to each scenario. Focus on the factors that influenced their decision; for instance, did they decide for practical reasons or because they believed it was the correct moral decision? Focus on the differences between practical and moral reasons and question how they would feel about having to make a practical decision that may not (in their view) be morally correct. Examine the moral value lost in each scenario, such as in Scenario 3: 'Would you feel ashamed, worried, regretful about your decision to take the first-class ticket?' or 'Would you worry about the implications for the person who gave you the ticket?' Then look at less common responses and probe these decisions – sometimes, these will involve additional aspects not necessarily outlined in the original scenario. Ask students if they considered different contexts and how these impacted their decision, such as in Scenario 4 where you could have been rushing for the plane because you have a seriously ill relative that you need to return home to. Finally, invite students to consider difficult choices they had to make in their own lives and how they made those choices. Explain that, if students wish to tell the class about their decisions, they are welcome to do so, but they do not need to. In follow-on questions, focus on the factors that made each decision difficult and how they ultimately made their choice.

The second exercise – the Lifeboat activity – examines stereotyping through the lens of a moral dilemma. It aims to enable students to recognise that everybody is entitled to human dignity, and to also understand how stereotypes can affect how people treat others. Begin the exercise by reading the scenario on **Worksheet 7.2** to students. The students then read the short pieces of information about the 10 characters. Working in small groups, the students must decide which six passengers they will save. They will do so by ranking each passenger, with the top six passengers given a place on the lifeboat. Finally, they must justify their decision.

When taking feedback, you might create a continuum on the board (noting 1 to 10) and ask a member of each group to show the ranking they had made. This will probably show a significant amount of conformity at the extremes, but perhaps not at the centre. Ask firstly how each group decided on the ranking; then ask whether the other groups agreed or whether they had different views. Ask what factors made it difficult to decide. Students may identify issues such as insufficient information or having to decide whether people were honest in the information they provided. Ask whether everyone in the group agreed and if not, how they came to a group decision. Finally, remind students that one of the purposes of exploring moral dilemmas is to discover their capacity to engage students in critical discussion and to rationalise and justify actions.

In the Lifeboat exercise, begin the drama element with the appearance at a press conference of the six characters who were saved. Ask each character to outline their story and allow no more than a minute to do so. Then, when each character has spoken, open the floor to questions from the reporters (all the other students). Students must use a microphone (you can improvise using a ruler or pencil case) before they can speak. The teacher, as presenter, may also call on students to speak – this helps prevent students talking over each other. As the activity is improvised, the questions will be spontaneous. However, it is important to encourage a range of different question types, such as:

- Fact recall;
- Probing;
- Causes, effects and solutions;
- Probable and possible outcomes;
- Emotional impact.

You may need to play 'devil's advocate' here, or to model some question types.

Having completed the first stage of the exercise, ask the first characters to return to the audience and choose four new characters to represent the four people who were left to drown. Fortunately, it is posited, they were later rescued and, in the news conference, they get the opportunity to describe their traumatic experience. Use the same format for this news conference as the one you used in the first. We have found that the second news conference is often more interesting, as the students may bring more information to bear, including how the information used to deny them entry to the lifeboat may have been inaccurate; or how some of the characters who were saved may have misrepresented themselves. Finally, hot seat two students to act as crew members. Ask them to explain how they made their decision to save the six people and how hearing the previous testimonies now has impacted them.

Afterwards, encourage all the students to carefully reflect on this exercise. Possible guiding questions include:

- How did it feel to be the character you played?
- What did you learn from playing this role?
- How does this character's experience differ from your experience?
- Would this experience influence how you view other people's experiences?

'Writing in role' – which uses such tasks as diary entries, letters, blogs or newspaper reports – offers an opportunity to deepen students' reflections and understandings of global citizenship issues. Ask the students to write an account of the lifeboat activity from the viewpoint of the character that they played. Suggest using either a diary entry or a letter to a close friend or family member. Students who were in the hot seat could tell their story and what they thought of the questions that were posed to them. Encourage the students to revisit the decision they made and to note how they now felt when they saw the different characters interviewed. For those who were in the hot seat, ask them to identify the more challenging questions that they were asked, record the responses they gave and, now that they have reflected on these questions, what responses would they give if asked again.

Bouchard (2002, p.416) suggests the following narrative structure:

- What did you decide to do? Why? (Students affirm the decision/action);
- Do you think that this was the best thing to do under the circumstances? Why? (Students evaluate their decision/action and justify the evaluation);
- What did you learn from this experience? How do you see things now? (Students reflect on life lessons and actions that they can take from this experience).

Reflection

In the reflective element of the lesson, it is important to consider firstly how circumstances can affect how some people are treated by others. While everyone has a right to human dignity, people do not experience it equally. Often, Others may be viewed (directly or indirectly) as inferior. Ask the students to consider again the factors that impacted how people were treated in these exercises. Possible questions include:

- Were these reasons valid reasons?
- Why do you think these reasons were used?
- Would you change your action? Why/why not?

When considering other situations where people are effectively and affectively judged, try to identify areas where there are conflicting views and how, as a result, some people are disadvantaged over others. We have found that students are often familiar with war situations, but you might also encourage a wide range of responses that include social, as well as political, issues. Focus on the factors used to judge how people are differentially viewed in these situations.

Finally, ask the students to reflect on the difficulties involved in decision-making. Ask them to consider the morally correct outcome, in addition to the most 'rational' outcome. Examine the factors that they view as 'reasonable' to consider in decision-making. Look at the factors that make decisions especially difficult, such as when they have a serious impact on the person or when an urgent decision is needed. You may use the Covid-19 pandemic as an example to show how decisions were taken in the public interest, but how these decisions may have had an impact on individuals and their families. In conclusion, ask the students what they have learned from this lesson and how it might impact their future decision-making.

Lesson Plan 7: Moral Dilemmas

Purpose of this lesson (learning objectives):
To recognise the various factors that influence how people view others' human dignity and to raise awareness that everyone has human dignity.

Teacher Materials:
- **Worksheets 7.1** and **7.2**
- Classroom with four single seats

Format:
- Individual reflection
- Paired discussion
- Small group discussion
- Hot-seating exercise

	Activity	Let's talk about it
Lead in **What is a dilemma?**	Ask students to explain in their own words what they understand by the term 'dilemma'? What then do they think is meant by a 'moral dilemma'? Individually, ask the students to read **Worksheet 7.1** and, for each scenario, to note what they would do and why. Then ask the students to work in pairs to compare and contrast their answers. In a class discussion, ask the students what their most common responses to each scenario were. Focus especially on why they chose the responses.	How many people decided based their own belief that they were doing the morally right thing? How many people decided based on what they thought would be the most practical outcome? Were some decisions harder to make? If so, why do you think they were? Can you identify any scenario where you personally had to make a difficult choice and how did you make your decision?
The Lifeboat activity	Read the scenario outlined in **Worksheet 7.2** with the class. Then ask the students to work in small groups to identify the six people they would pick to get a place in the lifeboat. Within the group, they must discuss the reasons for their choice and note them on the sheet.	What factors in each person's life did you use to make your decision? What was the hardest part of the decision? Did everyone in the group agree? How did you reach a group decision? What have you learned from this exercise?

	Activity	Let's talk about it
Hot Seating	For the hot-seating exercise, emphasise that the students playing the roles of the passengers and crew will need to provide more information on the people and consider different aspects of their lives that were not considered in making the original decision – for instance, something beneficial they had done or somebody who would have been severely impacted by their absence, or in the case of somebody who was saved, something negative that was not known about them but may have influenced the decision if it was. Imagine that the six characters who were saved are appearing at a news conference. Choose students to roleplay the six candidates and seat them on six chairs facing the rest of the class. Ask the class to play the role of reporters and question them on their experience and why they think they were chosen. Then imagine that the four characters who were left behind were later rescued and are telling their story in another news conference. Choose students to roleplay these four people and seat them on four chairs facing the class. Ask the class to play the role of reporters and question them about their experience and why they think they were not chosen. Finally, pick two people to play the ship's crew and seat them facing the class. Then ask the class members as news reporters to question how they decided to save some people and leave others to drown.	Did you learn anything else about these characters that may have changed your decision? What assumptions had you made about each of the characters? What do you learn about how you make decisions from this exercise?
Writing in role	Ask the students to write a diary or a letter to a close friend or family member where they recount their character's experience of the lifeboat activity. Emphasise that the account must mention how they felt at each point. Encourage them to include how they felt after witnessing the news conferences.	Why is a diary account or a letter to a close friend or family member a useful exercise here? Do you feel that you have a better understanding of how the people involved in this story would feel? How would this lesson influence how you engage with other people?

Time to think
What have you learned about how people view the human dignity of others? Can you think of other situations where people are judged on a range of different features? In these moral dilemmas, several factors influenced how the decisions were made, such as the morally correct position or the most logical outcome. What does this tell you about decision-making?

Worksheet 7.1: Moral Dilemmas

Scenario 1

Imagine you're at the wheel of a railway trolley and the brakes have failed. You're approaching a fork in the track at top speed. On the left side, five rail workers are fixing the track. On the right side, there is a single worker. If you do nothing, the trolley will bear left and kill the five workers. The only way to save their lives is to take the responsibility for changing the trolley's path by hitting a switch. This action will kill the other worker.

What would you do?

Scenario 2

Imagine that you are watching the runaway trolley from a footbridge. This time, there is no fork in the track, but five workers are on it, facing certain death. But you happen to be standing next to a big man. If you push him off the footbridge, he will fall on the track and stop the trolley.

Do you wilfully kill one man, or do you allow five people die?

Scenario 3

You are checking in for a flight when the person at the counter accidentally gives you a boarding pass for a first-class seat. Your ticket is for economy.

Do you point out the mistake?

Scenario 4

You are running down a crowded corridor in the airport, trying to catch a flight that's about to leave. Suddenly an elderly woman in front of you slips and falls hard.

Do you stop to help, knowing that you'll miss your plane?

Scenario	What would you do?	Why?
1		
2		
3		
4		

Based on *Whose Life Would You Save?* (Zimmer, 2004)

Worksheet 7.2: The Lifeboat Dilemma

A luxury ship on a cruise in the Caribbean Sea has gone on fire and is sinking four kilometres off Barbados. Your group are the only officers left. There are 10 passengers and only six places in the lifeboat. Your group must decide which six passengers to save. Rank them in order from top to bottom choice and write a reason for your decision.

Person	Rank	Reason for their ranking
John is a lifeguard. He is 21 and is very fit. He is studying to be a doctor and has finished top of his class for the past three years.		
Sam is a 63-year-old recently widowed former builder. He has been forced to retire because he has developed emphysema, due to his smoking addiction.		
Wilma is a 50-year-old member of the cleaning staff on the ship. She has been in treatment twice for drug addiction, but says that she has overcome this problem.		
Sonya is a 32-year-old model. She came on the cruise to recover from a series of recent cosmetic operations.		
Eliot is a hedge fund manager and has made millions from his job. He brought Sonya on the trip, but his wife does not know.		
Laila is a cosmetics influencer on social media. She thinks she might be six weeks pregnant.		
Bruce is an 80-year-old retired paramedic. He is in good health apart from his poor eyesight.		
Jason is 18. He was recently released from juvenile detention for stealing from his elderly neighbours.		
Deborah is a 25-year-old primary school teacher. She recently married Eric. She came on the cruise as part of her honeymoon.		
Eric is Deborah's 27-year-old husband. He is an illegal immigrant but hopes that he will now become legal through his marriage to Deborah.		

LESSON 8:
MIGRATION

Migration has always been and continues to be a feature of human behaviour. There are many different reasons why migration occurs – it can be voluntary or forced, internal or transnational, permanent/circular or seasonal, and it can be undertaken for economic, social, religious or cultural reasons (Quaynor & Murillo, 2018). The United Nations High Commissioner for Refugees (UNHCR, *n.d.*) distinguishes between the terms 'refugee' and 'migrant' and recommends that the two terms not be conflated to avoid undermining the protections to which refugees (in particular) are legally entitled. The term 'refugee' refers to people who are "outside their own country because of a threat to their lives or freedom" (see https://www.unhcr.org/ie/about-us). Refugees are defined and protected by international law, whereas 'migrants' are not. The term 'migrant', therefore, has tended to refer to 'voluntary' rather than 'forced' migration. The organisation, Teaching Immigration in European Schools (TIES, *n.d.*), note that emigration was the dominant movement from Europe from the 1500s to the 1940s – this was due to colonisation, trade and the need to escape poverty. However, this trend has changed since the post-World War II period when Europe instead became a destination for immigrants – both for immigrant workers and refugees. Similarly, migration patterns have changed in other areas of the world, with emigration now being more prevalent than immigration in Latin America, and with the Gulf States experiencing larger numbers of immigrants, for example. In recent years, Ireland too has seen a positive immigration rate. By 2024, Ireland's population had reached 5,380,300, of which 15.5% were non-Irish-born citizens and, in the 12 months to the end of April 2024, 58% of immigrants into Ireland came from outside the EU and the UK (CSO, 2024). Interestingly, Ireland's emigration figure in 2024 (estimated to be 69,000 people) was the highest since 2015 (*ibid.*).

Guidance

Quaynor & Murillo (2018) highlight the importance of GCE and its capacity to demonstrate to receiving communities the common bonds that they share with migrants and the societies from which they come. In reality, the arrival of migrants in receiving communities often can lead to calls for a nationalistic-focused citizenship education which actually emphasises differences and teaches that people who 'do not fit' (in this case, a narrow nationalistic definition) cannot be regarded as equal citizens. Quaynor & Murillo (2018) suggest that receiving communities have two options to adopt in relation to their treatment of newly arrived migrants. They can follow an assimilationist policy, whereby migrants are encouraged to discard their own culture and fully embrace that of the receiving country. Such a nationalistic-focused citizenship education position, as highlighted in **Lesson 5**, is deemed (from a critical liberal perspective) to be inadequate (for example, Banks, 2008). Alternatively, receiving communities can follow and promote a policy that *includes* multiple communities (in tandem with 'their' own shifting identities). With the former option, people from migrant cultures are taught that their culture does not matter as much, or at all – that their community identity brings little or no benefit to the host community. With the latter option, people from diverse cultures learn to see that their culture is valued. In essence, *both* communities can learn about the advantages (as well as the challenges) that migration brings to the host society.

Moreover, *teaching* migration – for example, teaching this topic in a dedicated GCE unit of learning or integrating it in a subject discipline – is essential for both migrant and non-migrant students (Quaynor & Murillo, 2018). Indeed, to ignore the reality of migration is to miss an important 'teachable moment' (as Paulo Freire would term it); it could even lead to a diminished state of 'sense and sensibility' (O'Brien, 2016), with students being misinformed and/or becoming more fearful about new world realities. At a deeply human level, students may feel that host community membership somehow confers more value to an individual than being categorised as a non-legal citizen. Reciprocally, students from diverse cultures may perceive themselves to hold lesser value. Thus, to confront such a diminished state of 'sense and sensibility' (O'Brien, 2016), it is important that teachers, alongside other learners in the classroom, acknowledge and act on 'migration'. We hope that this lesson inspires you to do just that.

Activities

The UNHCR (2021) urges caution before teaching about migration, refugees or asylum seekers. They suggest discussing the topic in advance with students and including, where possible, ideas and feedback from the students themselves and/or their parents. In **Lesson 9**, we offer additional guidance on teaching about so-called 'sensitive' (though, essential) topics. To help with teaching about 'migration', we refer the reader to Rutter's work.

Rutter (2012, p.218) suggests a number of considerations in managing a dialogue about migration (see **Table 8.1**).

Lesson 8 begins by looking at the history of Irish migration. We have found that, by beginning to look at migration through an Irish lens, students may come to a deeper understanding of other migrants' experiences; it also enables them to more likely question stereotypes and critique its impact on Others. A possible starting point could be to briefly outline a personal example of migration, such as your (or a family member's or friend's) experience of migration. Such examples may involve summer jobs in a different country, where the benefits of such experiences can be highlighted. In speaking of one's experiences, the abstract concept of 'migration' can be personalised, and students can come to see the advantages of migration and how it can be viewed as something positive. We suggest that you only do this if you are comfortable about discussing your personal story.

Table 8.1: Managing a Discussion about Migration

Preparation

Before embarking upon lessons or workshops, it is essential to meet with the students to learn what their perceptions about migration are. This enables the teacher or group leader to understand students' concerns, knowledge gaps and value bases and to personalise and negotiate the topics for subsequent workshops.

Step 1: Creating a safe space for debate

Using fun icebreaking activities, this step focuses on creating the open space in which students can feel safe and free to debate. The teacher focuses on establishing the trusting conditions that are conducive to a community of enquiry being formed. Facilitators cannot create this space on their own; they need the help of all participants to ensure that no one is left out and that each person feels able to share his or her own point of view. It is useful to highlight challenges in creating the right atmosphere, such as listening attentively to each other, working as a team, staying focused and thinking hard.

Step 2: Engagement with different perspectives – presenting the stimulus

Participants are introduced to different and 'logical' perspectives about migration. The perspectives should present different angles on the issue; these can be taken from a variety of sources and can be presented in different formats, such as newspaper articles, cartoons, stories, pictures and online videos.

Step 3: First thoughts – clarifying and sharing points of view

Participants work in pairs to consider and respond to the different sources of information about migration (identifying mainstream and non-mainstream perspectives). Participants can be provided with some reflective questions that help them to consider their personal responses to the stimuli provided. Handouts also can be used to invite participants to individually draw and/or write down thoughts on the materials.

Step 4: The group dialogue

Questions that critically explore migration (which can be generated by the students and/or the facilitator) are explored by the whole group. During this group dialogue, the facilitator's role is to try and encourage the participants to explore different angles and points of view on the topic and allow them to make their own considered judgements.

Step 5: Enquiry activity (optional)

Commonly, the group dialogue generates new questions that the participants wish to research and enquire about further. This can lead to an independent research project or to student-generated perspectives which can serve as stimuli for another workshop. Alternatively, a problem-solving task can be devised which gives participants an opportunity to apply the skills and knowledge gained in the dialogical process to a real-life or simulated situation that necessitates responsible decision-making.

Step 6: Last words – closing the space

Participants are invited to reflect on their participation and learning and provide some feedback, either written or verbal, concerning what they have learned about migration, about themselves, about others and about the learning process. What they now know and feel about 'migration' is important to ascertain.

Ask students to look at **Worksheet 8.1** which shows three pictures that present different representations of Irish people. The first shows a stereotypical image of a drunken Irishman, caricatured with an ape-like face; the second shows a drawing of a 'coffin ship' that would have taken poor Irish emigrants across the Atlantic at the time of the Great Famine; and the third is a job advertisement where the infamous caveat 'No Irish need apply' is used. Use the questions on the worksheet to raise students' awareness that the question of emigration was a pertinent issue for the Irish in the past and that representations of 'the Irish' were often highly unflattering. The third image, for example, demonstrates how such representations had an impact on whether Irish emigrants were eligible to apply for work. The questions move from identifying how the Irish were treated to looking at why these images were produced, and to how they make students *feel*.

An extension question could be to ask if students know of any family members who migrated and, if so, to where. While they may mention many different destinations, we have found that most students reference English-speaking countries such as the UK, USA, Australia, Canada and New Zealand. The obvious linguistic advantage of moving to these countries remains a key factor in choosing these locations – add to this the need for more workers – but there is also the social capital factor that migrants may acquire by travelling to places where there is a ready-made community of expatriates. This latter feature of migration, referred to as 'chain migration', is commonly recognised (Quaynor & Murillo, 2018).

Question students on why Irish people travel where they do and the social capital that is provided in these locations. Now ask them whether the same is true for other migrants from other parts of the world.

The questions presented in the *Let's talk about it* section aim to identify whether the images from **Worksheet 8.1** are still used to represent the Irish; why the students might consider them as inappropriate; and why such images used to represent different groups are no longer prevalent. Students have looked at stereotypes in **Lesson 6** and the sources of many stereotypes in **Lesson 5**. Encourage students to identify how these 'negative stereotypes' develop and their impact on local and new communities. Question why representations may have changed – this could involve such causal factors as greater wealth, employment, education and greater levels of equal opportunity. Moreover, it is important to state that using such negative representations – and the attendant exclusion of any group from applying for jobs, for example – are no longer acceptable or even legal in many countries, including Ireland. Finally, ask whether everything that appears on **Worksheet 8.1** has changed and, if not, where such negative representations may still be present (you might consider the use of social media here, for example).

A possible extension exercise is to examine the history of immigration in Ireland, mentioning groups such as the Celts, Vikings, Normans or English and Scottish settlers during the plantations. The aim of this exercise is to put contemporary immigration into perspective and demonstrate that there is no such thing as a single 'Irish' identity, since it has historically included many different migrant group bringing elements of their own culture that becomes another part of Irish culture. You could reference, for example, how the Vikings were responsible for the first towns in Ireland, or how the Normans brought us our great castles. If you do not use this activity, please keep in mind that Ireland has always experienced immigration; that the mixing of immigrant and native cultures have redefined many times what is meant by 'the Irish culture'; and that overly simplistic viewpoints that say that migration dilutes Irish culture are challenged by 'a history still in the making'.

Look now at some more recent examples of Irish migration. Ask the students to examine **Worksheet 8.2**. Begin by asking how many people the students can recognise (the answers are given in **Table 8.2**). Then ask what they all have in common: one obvious response is that they are all Irish and/or that they have achieved great success by travelling and working outside Ireland.

Table 8.2: What Do They Have in Common?

Person	Famous for...
Michael Fassbender	actor
Graham Norton	television host, comedian and writer
Saoirse Ronan	actress
Niall Horan	singer
Samuel Beckett	writer
Brendan O'Carroll	comedian and actor

Because these people are internationally famous, they are often the first people that come to mind when other people think about 'the Irish'. Question how they could impact other people's thinking on what it means to be Irish and, secondly, question whether this international representation is a good or a bad thing.

We suggest that students work in small groups for the stereotyping activity. Ask them to look at **Worksheet 8.3** and to circle any word that may be used to describe migrants. Then ask them to discuss the questions on the worksheet. Students will explain why the word is used, who they have heard using the word and how they think this word would make a migrant feel. The words are a combination of four positive and six negative adjectives. In taking feedback, begin with one group, ask for one word they chose, ask who uses it, ask the reasons why it is used and how they think a migrant would feel to be described by this word. Ask the other groups whether they had the same word and, for those who did, ask them whether they had alternative people, reasons or feelings to present to the class. Then move to the next group and ask for another word and work through the same questions. Continue asking groups until each group has suggested a word. This exercise should help students to identify that those people who are most negative in their views may have less knowledge of, or interaction with, migrants. It is important to identify how positive words also are linked to migrants, for example 'skilled' (perhaps the students may have chosen such words because they have interacted with migrant workers in hospitals, for example?). The positive terms are more likely to have been chosen by students who have more knowledge of, or have had some interaction with, migrants. Recall how negative representations of Irish emigrants led employers in the past to have such negative views of them that they were often precluded from applying for jobs. Ask students about the impact of any of these stereotypical words on migrants – what would happen if they were held and practised by people, such as employers, landlords or teachers?

Before beginning the next activity (Poem on Refugees), we recommend that you, once again, consider your class profile and the need to treat the topic in a sensitive manner. This exercise has a particular focus – it is centred on 'forced migration'. The poem *Refugees* by Brian Bilston (2022) on **Worksheet 8.4** is cleverly written to appear like a series of negative tropes about refugees on a first reading. However, as you will see, by reading it backwards (upwards, starting with the last line), it offers a very different perspective. We recommend that you read the poem to the class 'from the top to the bottom' of the poem. Then ask students how the poem made them feel and what negative words and stereotypes they identified about migrants in the poem. Use these questions to focus on the feelings these descriptions elicit and how negative stereotypes are used to create this 'affect'. Once you have discussed the poem re-read it, but this time 'begin with the bottom line and read upwards'. We suggest you ask how this version of the poem now makes students feel and whether it provides a response to any of the negative stereotypes they had already identified. A key point to emphasise is how words can be hurtful and how the same words can also be used to present an important counterargument. Finally, question students as to why they think Brian Bilston wrote the poem in this manner.

Next, ask students to read the quotes on **Worksheet 8.5**, to work in small groups to choose one quote and then to answer the questions that follow. The exercise should make it clear that there are a range of reasons for migration, forced and voluntary, and there are important reasons why people need international protection. Students should be able to identify why people migrate from home, that the alternatives are not always practical and that there are also problems that occur when migrants move.

We suggest that students work in small groups or pairs to complete this activity. Each group/pair should choose a quote and analyse it using the questions on **Worksheet 8.5**. You may allocate a quote to each group or allow the students choose their own. In taking feedback, begin with one pair/group, ask for one quote they chose and go through the questions related to that quote. Ask the other pairs/groups whether they had the same quote and, for those who did, whether they had alternative responses. Then move to the next pair/group and ask for another quote and work through the same questions. Continue asking pairs/groups until each pair/group has suggested a quote. We recommend that you complete the exercise by asking what the students have learned from the variety of responses they have given.

The purpose of this activity on migrants at work in **Worksheet 8.6** is to demonstrate the economic benefits that migrants bring to a country. We suggest that you begin by showing the video, *A Day without Migrants* (YouTube: https://youtu.be/DVwrkYnKZT4). The video shows the impact of not having migrant workers – there is no sound engineer, no bus driver, no chef or waiter, the cellist is not available to play at the orchestra and, more seriously (evidenced by the change in tone with the music moving from light and pleasant to sombre), there is no medical staff when the child is sick. Throughout the video, anti-migrant literature is shown to explain why there are no migrant workers.

We suggest that you ask the students to then read the migrants' accounts on **Worksheet 8.6** and to examine the statistics on migrants at work in the EU *before* beginning a class discussion on the information they have just looked at. In the class discussion, ask the students what they learned about the benefits that migrants bring to a country, the challenges migrants continually face and what they think could be done to lessen some of these. The aim of the questions is to show that migrants bring economic benefits to a country and that, without migrant workers, many essential areas of the economy would simply not be able to operate.

You could extend this activity by asking questions that probe whether they know migrants who provide such essential services.

In running a whole class discussion, we recommend that you consider the guidelines in **Table 8.3**.

Reflection

In the reflective element of this lesson, it is important to consider the range of circumstances that can cause people to leave their own country. Examine the reasons why people are not aware of, or understand, the reasons for migration. In exploring the Irish context, you could reference different periods of emigration, such as during the famine from 1845, or the 1950s, or the 1980s, or the 2008 to 2013 period. Remind students of the causes of Irish emigration, where Irish emigrants went and ask what they have learned from doing this activity.

Ask the students to consider the benefits migrants bring to a country and why these benefits are not always or immediately recognised. Examine the differences that having no migrants would make in their own local area. Ask the students to identify the supports that need to be put in place for migrants, how to change mindsets and what it says about us as global citizens that such problems and challenges persist.

Finally, question the students about whether their thinking on migration has changed after this lesson and, if so, *how*. Allow an opportunity for students to raise any concerns they may have on completion of the lesson. Suitable questions for helping students reflect on their view of migration could include:

- How would you convince somebody who was opposed to migration of the benefits it brings?
- How would you respond to somebody in your group who makes negative comments about migrants that are not based on evidence?

Table 8.3: Guidelines for Whole Class Discussions

Be prepared for the rapid pace of class discussions. Planning questions in advance helps you to control the flow of the discussion. Ask questions with several possible answers, as this helps develop the skill of identifying context. Rosenshine (2012), based on King (1994), suggests the following stems for questions that teachers might ask:
- How are _____ and _____ alike?
- What is the main idea of _____?
- What are the strengths and weaknesses of _____?
- In what way is _____ related to _____?
- Compare _____ and _____ with regard to _____.
- What do you think causes _____?
- How does _____ tie in with what we have learned before?
- Which one is the best _____, and why?
- What are some possible solutions for the problem of _____?
- Do you agree or disagree with this statement: _____?
- What do you still not understand about _____?

Expect pupils to justify their responses and back them up with evidence.
- Where did you hear that information?
- Where did you get those figures?

Avoid asking whether anybody has questions, instead use follow-up questions such as:
- Why?
- Can you mention any circumstances where...?
- What are the causes of this...?
- What are the impacts of this...?
- Can you suggest any solutions to this...?
- Your point is interesting, can you tell me a little more about what you mean by...?

Encourage the whole class to participate by using questions such as:
- What do the rest of you think about what _____ has just said?
- Is this statement correct?
- Do you agree/disagree?
- Would anyone like to say something more about this topic?
- Are there any other issues about this topic that we have not mentioned?

Make links to other topics:
- Have we discussed this issue already?
- Has this problem any links to other issues that we have discussed?
- How does this differ to _____?

Monitor the discussion:
- Avoid the topic of discussion moving away from the topic you want to discuss.
- Keep eye contact with all students during the discussion to keep all students on task and avoid potential disruption.
- Use non-verbal cues while other students are speaking, for instance nodding to a student to show that you will take their question next.
- Allow differences of opinion to develop as long as the students are respectful and supported by evidence.
- Make it clear to students that you are going to end the discussion by asking for final input.

Watch out for indications of problems (Davis, 2009):
- Excessive hair splitting or nit-picking.
- Repetition of points.
- Private conversations.
- Students taking sides and refusing to compromise.
- Ideas being attacked before they are completely expressed.
- Apathetic participation.

Lesson Plan 8: Migration

Purpose of this lesson (learning objectives):
To identify the complex reasons for migration.

Teacher Materials:
Worksheets 8.1 to 8.6
Pens for sharing

Format:
- Small group learning
- Whole class discussion

	Activity	Let's talk about it
Lead in **What has the Irish experience of emigration looked like?**	Show the pictures from **Worksheet 8.1** and ask students to answer the questions on the worksheet.	Do you think these images are still used nowadays? In what ways are they inappropriate? Why do you think they may no longer be prevalent?
What does migration now mean for the Irish?	Show the pictures from **Worksheet 8.2** and ask students the following questions: • How many of these people can you name? • What do they have in common?	Are these people considered migrants? Why/why not?
Stereotyping activity	In small groups, ask students to look at the words on **Worksheet 8.3**. They can choose any of the words they think are used to describe migrants and then discuss the questions on the worksheet. Take feedback by asking each group one by one for a word they selected; then write the word on the board and ask the group's response to each. Invite other groups to suggest alternative responses they gave to the questions. When all the information is noted, it should become obvious that the most negative answers come when people have little interaction with migrants.	What do you notice about the people who use the most negative words? Can you think of any impact for migrants of using negative words?
Poem on Refugees	Read the poem *Refugees* by Brian Bilston (**Worksheet 8.4**) to the class. Ask the following questions: • How does this poem make you feel? • What negative words and stereotypes can you identify about migrants? Then read the same poem, beginning with the bottom line and reading upwards and ask the following questions. • How does this version of the poem make you feel? • Does it answer any of the negative stereotypes you identified already? • Why do you think Brian Bilston wrote the poem in this manner?	From your reading of this poem, what do you learn about how words can be used to convey different messages?

	Activity	Let's talk about it
Why do people migrate?	Ask the students to read the quotes on **Worksheet 8.5** and, in small groups, to choose one quote and answer the questions on the worksheet. Take feedback by asking each group one by one for a quote they selected; then ask the group's response to each question. Invite other groups to suggest alternative responses they gave to the questions.	What have you learned about migration from these quotes? What problems have you identified that can make migrants' lives difficult when they leave their own country?
Migrants at work	Begin by showing the students the video, *A Day without Migrants* (approximately two minutes duration – https://www.youtube.com/watch?v=DVwrkYnKZT4). Then ask the students to read the two migrants' stories on **Worksheet 8.6** and ask them to look at the EU statistics. Use the video, migrant accounts, and statistics to begin a whole class discussion.	What did you learn about the benefits migrants bring to a country? What challenges do migrants face? What do you think could be done to lessen some of these challenges? Do you know any migrants that provide an essential service? What would happen if these migrants were not available?

Time to think
How has the Irish experience of migration changed over time? Why has this happened and why is it now different to other migrants' experiences? What have you learned about the circumstances behind why people migrate? Why do you think that circumstances that drive people to migrate are often not well understood? Has your thinking about migration changed and, if so, how?

Worksheet 8.1: Historical Images of the Migrant Irish

Look at the three images below.

The first is a representation from an English magazine of an Irish man in the 19th century.

The second is of a so-called a 'coffin ship', unseaworthy ships that crossed the Atlantic Ocean bringing Irish emigrants to the USA. Many emigrants died of fevers they caught from other passengers on the voyage due to the overcrowded conditions.

The third is a job advertisement from an American newspaper, *The New York Times*, 10 November, 1854.

Thomas Nast, *A Cartoonist Depicts "The Usual Irish Way of Doing Things*, SHEC: Resources for Teachers, https://shec.ashp.cuny.edu/items/show/640.

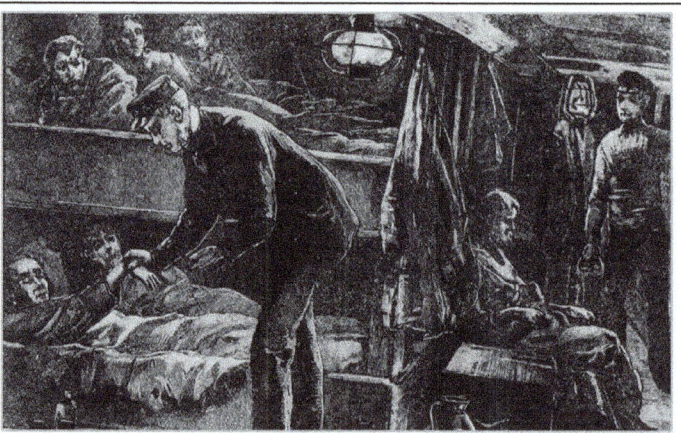

On Board an Emigrant Ship at the Time of the Irish Famine, A.D. 1846, https://www.irishcentral.com/opinion/others/irish-famine-coffin-ships.

GIRL WANTED – In a small private family – a young girl, 14 or 15 years old, either American or German, to take care of a young child. She must have good references. Wages 43 a month. No Irish need apply. Call at No. 89 McDougal St.

- Are you familiar with any of these images or the history behind them?
- Why do you think the Irish people were treated in this manner?
- Who do you think created these images?
- Why were they made?
- How do they make you feel?

Worksheet 8.2: Modern-day Irish Migrants

- How many of these people can you name?
- What do they have in common?

Worksheet 8.3: Labels

Circle any of the words below that are used to describe migrants.
- Can you name any people who use this word?
- Write a few words that you think explain why they use this word.
- Write how you think this word would make a migrant feel.

Worksheet 8.4: Refugees by Brian Bilston

They have no need of our help
So do not tell me
These haggard faces could belong to you or me
Should life have dealt a different hand
We need to see them for who they really are
Chancers and scroungers
Layabouts and loungers
With bombs up their sleeves
Cut-throats and thieves
They are not
Welcome here
We should make them
Go back to where they came from
They cannot
Share our food
Share our homes
Share our countries
Instead let us
Build a wall to keep them out
It is not okay to say
These are people just like us
A place should only belong to those who are born there
Do not be so stupid to think that
The world can be looked at another way

Worksheet 8.5: Why Do People Migrate?

- People in my town have disappeared and then been found murdered.
- Boys from my village have been forced to become child soldiers. I want my son to be safe.
- The education system is not good in my country.
- I am a blogger who has criticised the government.
- It is illegal for me to speak my language.
- I want to see the world and experience other cultures.
- Military service is compulsory in my country. I do not want to serve in the army.
- My uncle has been jailed for taking part in a protest.
- There is a civil war in my country
- 40% of young people are unemployed here.
- It is illegal for me to practise my religion.
- The government gives the good jobs to party members.
- I will gain experience in my job that I can't get at home.

Choose one quote and answer the following questions.

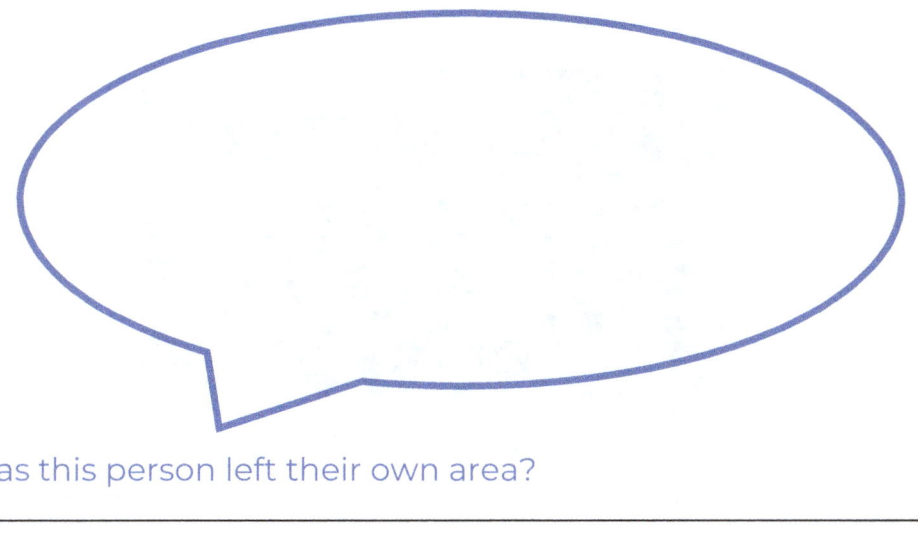

Why has this person left their own area?
_____
_____
_____

Is this an example of voluntary or forced migration? Explain your answer.
_____
_____
_____

Does this issue affect many people?
_____
_____
_____

Can you suggest any alternatives to migration for this person?
_____
_____
_____

Can you give any reason why people do not opt for these alternatives?
_____
_____
_____

Mention three problems these people may face when they leave their own country.
_____
_____
_____

Worksheet 8.6: Migrants at Work

Source: https://www.youtube.com/watch?v=DVwrkYnKZT4.

Lola Gonzalez, originally from Panama, works as a Retail Manager in County Leitrim. Lola is one of the participants in the Immigrant Council's Migrant Electoral Empowerment Programme, training migrants in the fundamentals of Irish politics. For Lola, settling in to her new life in Ireland without existing social and support networks made her sympathetic to the isolation many newcomers to Ireland feel. Her solution was to throw herself into her local community, joining local groups and volunteering her time for causes that matter to her.

Lola acknowledges that for many migrants it can be difficult adjusting the lifestyle here: "Some migrants will have a language barrier if they've another language as their first. Transportation can be an obstacle since Ireland is a country of cars and the public transportation system isn't well developed. Not every migrant will have the finances to own a car or have a driver's license. Not having access to services can be another obstacle, since you're not familiar on how to navigate the public systems in place".

Lola's community involvement makes her passionate about ensuring migrant representation at all levels of Irish society. "I feel that sometimes minority groups fail to be heard as no one is representing them where the big decisions are made. I hope to see more migrants take up roles of leadership so others see they can do so as well. I want to live in a community of inclusion and where migrants are treated as part of the society they call home."

Lola loves her life in rural Leitrim. "I love the tranquillity. I enjoy the unspoiled nature and slower pace of life. I like that most people know one another in towns. It creates more of a community spirit and a closeness that cities are missing. I have come to know people in my town through my job and volunteering in local groups. I think that in the current environment never has this being more important."

Adapted from Lola's account on https://www.immigrantcouncil.ie/story/lola-gonzalez

Maury, like many other Venezuelan migrants and refugees, left her country in the hopes of building a better future for herself and her family. Maury decided to leave Venezuela when her income as a doctor proved to be too little to support her family. "I could not even afford food for the whole month, so I decided to look for a job in Chile," she explains.

Leaving her two sons and mother behind, Maury faced challenges settling into a new culture and waiting to get her medical qualifications recognised in Chile. She taught online Spanish classes for seven months, while she took a course that helped prepare her for exams to work in her host country. "When my qualifications were finally certified, I had a lot of satisfaction from a professional and financial point of view," she recalls. Maury now delivers the same course for other migrants who are in the same situation.

Chile, one of the wealthiest countries in South America, remains a destination for many Venezuelans looking for better job opportunities. As much as she loves her new life in Chile. Maury hopes to one day be reunited with her family in Venezuela.

Adapted from an account written by Gema Cortés, marcortes@iom.int. https://www.iamamigrant.org/stories/maury

In 2022, 9.93 million non-EU citizens were employed in the EU labour market, out of 193.5 million persons aged from 20 to 64, corresponding to 5.1% of the total.

Occupation	% of non-EU citizens employed	% of EU citizens employed
Cleaners and helpers	11.4	2.9
Construction workers (excluding electricians)	6.1	3.7
Food preparation assistants	2.6	0.6
Agricultural, fisheries and forestry workers	2.4	0.7
Teaching professionals	2.4	5.5
Health professionals	1.5	3.1

European Commission (2024).

Having watched the video, read the two migrants' stories and the EU statistics, answer the following questions.
- What did you learn about the benefits migrants bring to a country?
- What challenges do migrants face?
- What do you think could be done to lessen some of these challenges?

LESSON 9: SEEKING ASYLUM

Earlier in the *Handbook*, we mentioned how each lesson builds upon the next, how earlier discussions about 'identity', 'belonging' and 'home' are crucial in building critical awareness and understanding, and how engagement with these themes help us to better prepare for later, and deeper, discussions on global injustice issues, such as 'displacement' and 'forced migration'. We recommend that you recall this previous learning before beginning this lesson on 'Seeking Asylum'.

Guidance

You might begin by encouraging students (in small groups) to write down on large pieces of paper, the important learning lessons of 'identity', 'home' and 'belonging'. You could then ask the students to tear up their pages – this is a powerful way of demonstrating the physical sense of destruction or loss when these qualities are taken away from us and students can report back to the larger group the specifics of what is lost. For example, 'when our homes and identities are taken from me, I lose': My favourite place; my memories; family; 'togetherness'; my freedom; my creativity; my individuality; my 'uniqueness', etc.

Activities

In this lesson, it is important to examine the historical roots of the term 'refugee' (see **Lesson 1** for more on the dangers of Ahistoricism), specifically in the context of our collective postcolonial responsibility. In other words, we are offered an opportunity to explore *why* refugees are forced to migrate and *how* the Western world or Global North contributes, or has contributed throughout history, to this humanitarian situation. The objective of reading evocative poetry is not to wound or disturb us (and we need to discuss this point), it is to give *agency* to those often silenced. Through evocative poetry (and the creative arts generally), we can introduce students to the very real sense of loss, grief, vulnerability and risk felt by migrants, as well as the many nuances and complexities which surround someone labelled and identified as a 'refugee' (Chandra, 2020).

The exercises on 'The Whole Picture' (**Worksheet 9.1**) and 'Put Yourself in the Picture' (**Worksheet 9.3**) engage students in active, creative and participative learning. Such activities enable students to develop their curiosity, imaginative and creative thinking and build empathy. You can pause and reflect together on how we sometimes fail to see the whole picture, and why this may be.

In the activity 'Quick, Pack!' (**Worksheet 9.2**), students are invited to think of the collages they made about their own homes in an earlier lesson, and here they must choose what to bring and what to leave behind. Before this activity begins, it is important to provide a delicate 'trigger' for all students (some may be very sensitised to this topic). Safely and supportively, it will be important to reflect together on how someone feels when they must leave things behind, memories behind and people behind. Pause and reflect on how this might change a person and impact their wellbeing, their sense of identity and belonging. Allow students also to consider what they could do to help someone rebuild all that they have lost (with special attention being paid to the many different types of loss endured).

The 'Songs of Hope' activity allows students to work collaboratively and think of songs (lyrics and melodies) which are hopeful and which can bring people together. It is important to demonstrate to students that hope through renewed action is always possible and is worth collectively striving for.

'Home', the poem by Warsan Shire (2011) (**Worksheet 9.4**), is very evocative. It deliberately uses dehumanising language and engages with the most sensitive of topics. Teachers may use their own discretion if and when they engage this piece. If you are concerned about the suitability of content, then you might select an extract or two to analyse. For instance, you could focus primarily on the final stanza, using it as a springboard for discussion about the many reasons people are forced to leave their homes. If you decide to use the poem in its entirety, we suggest some ways to approach this. You can revert back to your class contract and everyone can be reminded about the importance of mutual respect and reflection. There are offensive words and sexual violence in this poem, so we suggest that you might discuss how, as a group, you wish to use certain terms (such as the n-word) and respectfully engage with sensitive real-life issues, such as gender violence. Building strong pedagogical relationships in the praxis classroom is critical, especially when exploring injustice issues which so often demonstrate and perpetuate violence (symbolic and real) against people. Know your own students, use your own integrity, be honest about content, preview the materials and prepare. This lesson highlights the significance of built-in reflection time and space in the GCE classroom which provides students with a much-needed opportunity to engage emotionally with injustice.

Warsan Shire was born in Kenya to Somali parents. She now lives and works as a writer and teacher in London. In 2009, she visited the abandoned Somali Embassy in Rome, where some refugees had taken sanctuary. In an interview, the poet informs the reporter that, the very night before her visit, she was told that a young Somali had jumped from its roof to his death. This devastating encounter made a lasting impression on the poet who felt compelled to write a poem which more accurately describes the harsh reality of life as an undocumented refugee in Europe. She explains how she wrote the poem to help anyone who has ever suffered grief or a trauma, similar to the one described in the poem (Shire, 2021). Even though this poem presents as 'raw' artwork, it strives to sensitise us to the voiceless; to provide a deeper sense of the refugee 'crisis'. Our students need to be protected from the harsh realities of the world but when they are prepared to know more about them, and when they are prepared to work together to confront them, they can positively contribute to a better world.

The activities about 'Direct Provision' (**Worksheet 9.7**) are an important reminder that injustices are both globally and locally relevant. Many students may never have heard of 'Direct Provision' (DP) before and may be shocked to discover that there are DP Centres in their own communities. Some students may reside in these Centres and/or know others who do so. These activities enable *all* students to understand that, in our own communities, we can take action to improve the quality of everyone's lives. In solidarity, students may join together to raise awareness about systems such as DP. They may organise community events that campaign for the genuine inclusion of asylum seekers, such as The Sanctuary Runners in Cork City (a local movement which promotes solidarity with asylum seekers, migrants and refugees through sport). There are opportunities too for whole school engagement, to work together as one community dedicated to nurture empathy, care and solidarity amongst everyone.

Reflection

By posing problems, asking more questions and enabling students to enter into dialogue with one another on themes which involve violence, racism and oppression, the teacher may begin to think of themselves as a mediator, facilitating discussion and leading dialogue. Being an effective dialogue leader involves developing particular knowledge, skills, values and actions. In Ira Shor's words:

To lead dynamic dialogue, teachers can develop some resources: their conceptual habits of mind, their capacity to do classroom research, their ability to listen carefully to students and to include them in reflecting on the dialogue underway, their skill in group dynamics, and their verbal creativity in posing problems for discussion. Teachers also need a commitment to democracy, which includes sharing authority with students. (Shor, 1992, p.112)

Table 9.1 provides some insights into how you can develop such 'habits', although, like all learning processes, this takes time. We suggest that you use this table to guide your own reflections – consider what you are doing well and what areas require more attention and action. You can also adapt these ideas to help your students create their own classroom charter which as we discussed earlier, establishes a safe, regulated, democratic environment.

Table 9.1: Developing as a Dialogue Leader

'Habits of Mind'	Practical Implementation
Persist	Some lessons will be easier than others; some groups will be more resistant than others; some days will be more challenging. You will get it right and you will get it wrong. Just keep going and keep trying. It is a process and it is absolutely worth it.
Be aware of impulsivity	Reflect on your lessons. Think about the challenges and the stresses and learn from them. Try to respond and be proactive rather than reactive.
Listen and understand with empathy	Pay attention to and do not dismiss another person's thoughts, feelings and ideas; seek to put yourself in the other person's shoes; tell others when you can relate to what they are expressing; hold thoughts at a distance in order to respect another person's point of view and feelings.
Thinking flexibly	You are capable of changing perspectives; always consider the input of others; generate alternatives; 'weigh up' options.
Thinking about thinking (metacognition)	Be aware of your own thoughts, feelings, intentions and actions; get to know that what you do and say affects others; be willing to consider the impact of choices on yourself and others.
Striving for accuracy and exploring multiple truths	Nurture a desire for researching facts and getting as close to the 'truth' as possible (this is made possible by exploring multiple truths).
Questioning and posing problems	Develop a questioning attitude – question yourself, question students and nurture an environment where questions are always generated.
Applying past knowledge to new situations	Consider one's own and others' prior knowledge and experiences. Apply knowledge beyond the situation in which it was learned.
Thinking and communicating with clarity and precision	Strive for clarity and accuracy when speaking and writing. Avoid generalisations, distortions, minimisations and deletions.
Gathering data through all senses	Stop to observe what you see; listen to what you hear; take note of what you smell; taste what you are eating; feel what you are touching. Use your senses to guide your development as a reflective practitioner.
Creating, imagining, innovating	Think about how something might be done differently from the 'norm'; propose new ideas; strive for originality.
Responding with wonderment and awe	Stay curious and intrigued. Allow yourself to be open to the 'little' and 'big' surprises in life.
Taking responsible risks	Be willing to try something new and different and do not be afraid of making mistakes or of 'coming up short'.
Finding humour	Laugh when appropriate and laugh at yourself when you can.
Thinking interdependently	Be willing to work with others and welcome their input and perspective; be willing to learn from others; and be willing to welcome agreement and disagreement.
Remaining open to continuous learning	Be open to new experiences to learn from; be proud and humble enough to admit when you don't know; welcome new information and multiple perspectives.

Source: Adapted from Costa (2000) *Describing 16 Habits of Mind* (https://www.habitsofmindinstitute.org/hear-art/).

Lesson Plan 9: Seeking Asylum

Purpose of this lesson (learning objectives):
To develop critical thinking and inference skills;
To challenge assumptions;
To build empathy and develop respect for people who are forced to leave home.

Teacher Materials:
Cropped photo stills (**Worksheets 9.1** and **9.3**), printed A4 or smaller – one per group of three or four learners
Large A3 (or larger) sheets of paper – one per group of three or four learners
Packing My Suitcase (**Worksheet 9.2**) – one per learner
The Swimmers movie (available to stream on Netflix)
Song lyrics: *Titanium* (https://www.canva.com/playlist-covers/templates/)

Format:
Individual, small group and whole class learning

	Activity	Let's talk about it
Lead in **The Whole Picture**	Organise learners into groups of three or four and give each group one of the cropped images, stuck on to a large sheet of paper. Ideally, each group should have a different image. Invite learners to imagine what is happening outside the frame Ask learners to work together in their groups to extend the picture by drawing around it. When they have finished, allow time for groups to circulate and look at and discuss the drawings of other groups. Finally, show learners the 'complete' photographs and compare these with learners' interpretations.	Why did you extend the picture in this way? What evidence did you use in the image to help you? Did you use any existing knowledge to help you? If so, what? Did you base your ideas on any assumptions, stereotypes or prejudices? If so, what? Where did these ideas come from? What similarities and differences were there between your extended pictures and the complete photographs?
Quick! Pack!	Give each student a copy of the suitcase template. (Alternatively, using cereal boxes, students can make a suitcase which opens and closes, on the inside of which they draw or write their items.) Ask them to think of five items they would take in their suitcase and draw or write them inside the image they have been given.	What would you take with you if you had to leave home? Why did you choose these items? Was it difficult to decide? Why/why not? What would you miss if you had to leave home (and perhaps never return). Consider other aspects as well as physical items: friends, community etc

	Activity	Let's talk about it
Put yourself in the picture	Ask learners to choose a photograph and think about what the person in it might be thinking. Learners could draw thought bubbles on sticky notes and add them to the photograph. This could be done individually or collaboratively in groups. Ask learners to imagine a conversation that they might be having with a person from the photograph. Speech bubbles could be written on sticky notes and added to the photograph. This idea could be developed by organising learners into pairs or groups of three and asking them to take on the roles of the characters and act out a conversation.	
Malak & the Boat	Play the YouTube video: https://youtu.be/1Uxip_SbGY8, (*Malak and the Boat – UNICEF's Unfairy Tales*, by Aedin Donnelly [1.57 minutes]). Ask the students to close their eyes and listen to the introductory music. Then ask them to answer the first two questions on Worksheet 9.5. Then play the video a second time, asking students to watch it closely, before they answer the remaining questions on the worksheet	
Misplaced by Conflict	Explain to the students that they are going to listen to Clip 2 of *The Outsiders* (O'Brien & Cassidy, 2014), in which two young people (Natasha and Minahil), talk about where they live (0.55-05.55 https://www.rte.ie/radio/doconone/666539-the-outsiders-our-teenage-life-behind-barriers). Distribute **Worksheet 9.6** to each student. Invite students to note the most important things they hear in the space provided on the worksheet. Invite students to pair up, discuss their notes, and record additional points their partner heard. Then, each student should draw a picture of the girls' accommodation, labelling each part of their drawing as appropriate. Invite students to pair up as before, to compare their drawings, and help each other to make additions.	
Home – Warsan Shire	Watch the YouTube video (Home / Warsan Shire https://www.youtube.com/watch?v=o_XKy5g9rX8 [2:55 mins]) and listen to the poem.	Which line stands out most to you and why? How does the poem make you feel? Why? Choose the most striking image from the poem and sketch it. Make a collage about the poet's interpretation of Home. Look back at the presentations/collages you made earlier about Home. Now, in small groups, make comparisons about any similarities or differences between your perspective

	Activity	**Let's talk about it**
		on home and the poet's perspective.
Direct Provision	Give each group a copy of **Worksheet 9.7.** Ask the groups to appoint a note-taker and a spokesperson who would like to feedback their collective answers when they return to the large group. Ask each group to collectively discuss and answer the questions, to the best of their ability/knowledge. Remember to reassure the group that there are no right or wrong answers, this is a learning process. You could focus on themes that emerge by noting them on the whiteboard. It is possible the following may emerge: Where people drew their information about Direct Provision; people with direct experience, media, social media, friends, family, education etc. Other words that may emerge; refugee, asylum seeker, Stamp 4, protection applicant.	What do you know about the Direct Provision system? Have you or anyone you know ever visited a Direct Provision centre? What do you think it is like to live in a Direct Provision centre? Do you think Direct Provision centres help the people who live there integrate and participate into Irish society? Why/why not? Do you think it would be hard to keep your identity, or to hold on to your hopes and dreams for a better future while living in a Direct Provision centre?
Deconstructed video	Play the *Deconstructed* video (5 minutes) (Olusanya, 2021) from YouTube. Give the group some time to reflect on the video and take some notes Ask the group how they feel after watching the video. Did anything surprise them? What stood out in the video for them?	What stands out for you when watching the video? What thoughts or feelings are emerging for you as you watch the video?

Time to think
How does the activity about seeing the whole picture relate to ideas about identity and making assumptions? Close your eyes for a minute, hold your suitcase and hold the five items in your mind. How would you feel if you were leaving your country with only these items?

Worksheet 9.1: The Whole Picture

Worksheet 9.2: Quick, Pack!

Packing my suitcase

Oxfam Education
www.oxfam.org.uk/education

Activity sheet

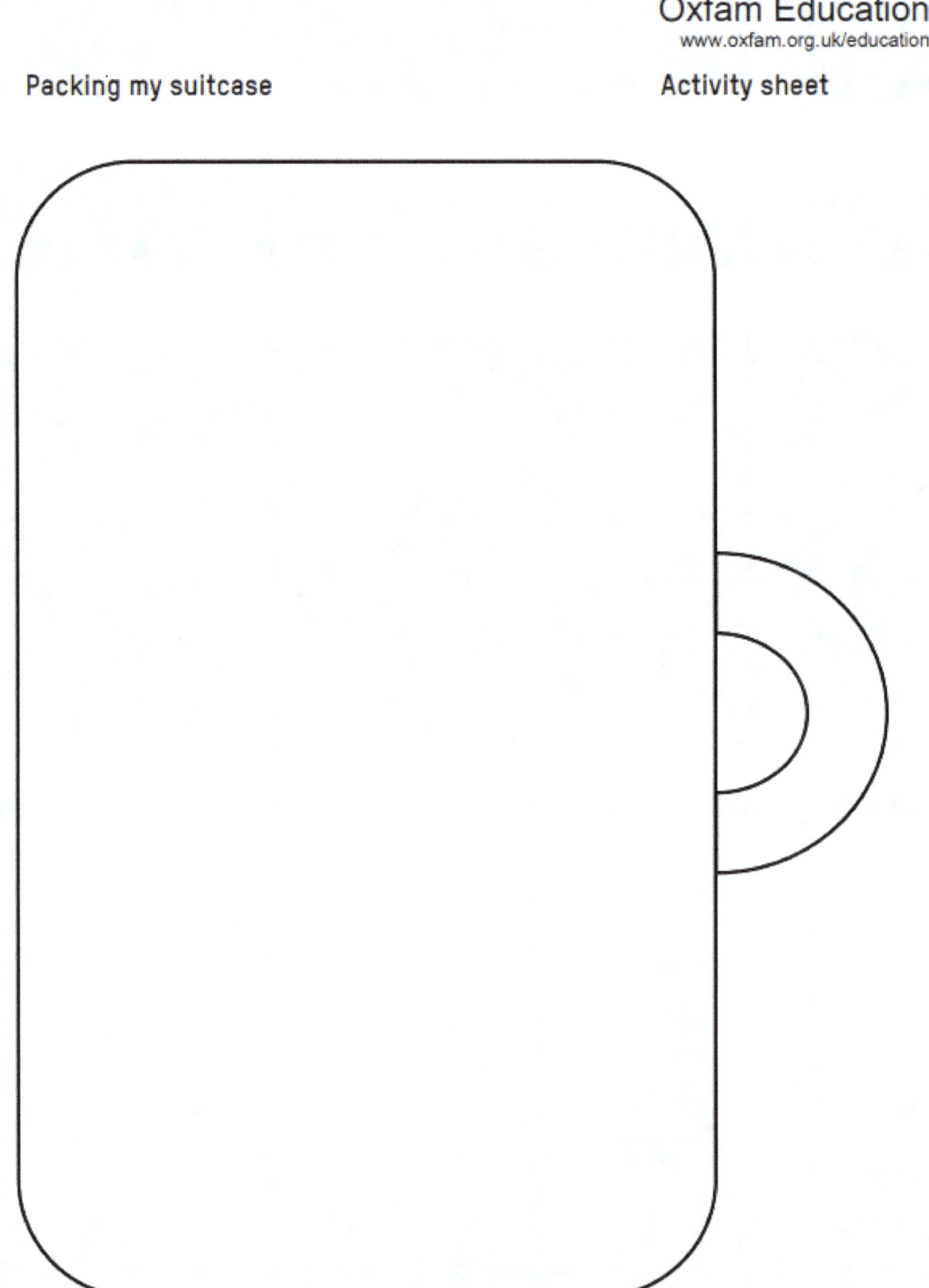

Worksheet 9.3: Put Yourself in the Picture

Worksheet 9.4: *Home* by Warsan Shire

no one leaves home unless
home is the mouth of a shark
you only run for the border
when you see the whole city running as well

your neighbors running faster than you
breath bloody in their throats
the boy you went to school with
who kissed you dizzy behind the old tin factory
is holding a gun bigger than his body
you only leave home when home
won't let you stay.

no one leaves home unless home chases you
fire under feet
 hot blood in your belly
 it's not something you ever thought of doing
until the blade burnt threats into
your neck
and even then you carried the anthem under
your breath
only tearing up your passport in an airport toilets
sobbing as each mouthful of paper
made it clear that you wouldn't be going back.

you have to understand,
that no one puts their children in a boat
unless the water is safer than the land
no one burns their palms
under trains
beneath carriages
no one spends days and nights in the stomach of a truck
feeding on newspaper unless the miles travelled
means something more than journey.
no one crawls under fences
no one wants to be beaten
pitied

no one chooses refugee camps
or strip searches where your
body is left aching
or prison,

because prison is safer
than a city of fire
and one prison guard
in the night
is better than a truckload of men who look like your father
no one could take it
no one could stomach it
no one skin would be tough enough

the
go home blacks
refugees

dirty immigrants
asylum seekers
sucking our country dry
niggers with their hands out
they smell strange
savage
messed up their country and now they want
to mess ours up
how do the words
the dirty looks
roll off your backs
maybe because the blow is softer
than a limb torn off

or the words are more tender
than fourteen men between
your legs or the insults are easier
to swallow
than rubble
than bone
than your child
body in pieces.
i want to go home,
but home is the mouth of a shark
home is the barrel of the gun
and no one would leave home
unless home chased you to the shore
unless home told you
to quicken your legs
leave your clothes behind
crawl through the desert
wade through the oceans
drown
save
be hunger
beg
forget pride
your survival is more important

no one leaves home until home is a sweaty voice in your ear
saying-
leave, run away from me now
I don't know what I've become
but i know that anywhere
is safer than here

https://www.youtube.com/watch?v=o_XKy5g9rX8
(link to video representation of the poem)

"Home" by Warsan Shire

Worksheet 9.5: Malak & the Boat

Close your eyes and listen to the introductory section of music score from the video, **Malak & the Boat**.

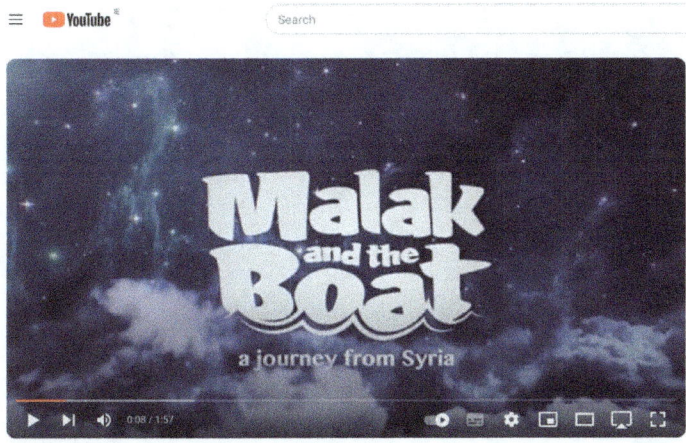

Malak and the Boat - UNICEF's Unfairy Tales

- How does this music make you feel?
- How do you picture the story which is about to unfold?

Write down your ideas and discuss in pairs.

Now watch the video in full.
- What do you see?
- How does the film director create a sense of fear?
- How does the narration compound this sense of fear?
- Did the ending surprise you? why?

Worksheet 9.6: The Outsiders

Listen to Clip 2 of **The Outsiders**, in which you will hear two girls, Natasha and Minahil, describe where they live.

ON YOUR OWN:
Listen carefully – then write down (in bullet points) what you heard.

NOW SHARE YOUR IDEAS WITH A PARTNER.
Write down things you partners heard that you didn't hear.

NEXT, AGAIN ON YOUR OWN, AND BASED ON WHAT YOU & YOUR PARTNER HEARD, DRAW WHAT YOU THINK THE ACCOMODATION CENTRE AND SURROUNDING AREA LOOKS LIKE:

NOW SHARE YOUR DRAWING WITH YOUR PARTNER & DISCUSS THE DIFFERENCES.

Source: https://www.worldwiseschoools.ie/wp-content/uploads/2018/03/APA_Outsiders_web.pdf?x73158.

Worksheet 9.7: Direct Provision

Has your opinion of Direct Provision and the protection process changed? How?

Do you understand the concept of 'deconstructed' put forward in the video?

Has this video changed your thoughts about people who have been or are in Direct Provision? How?

Can you understand how people in Direct Provision suffer from oppression?

In what ways do you think they suffer from stigma, self-stigma, low self-worth, hopelessness?

Can you understand how people may lose their own identity and become a label that is forced upon them? The struggles they may go through to fight to keep their own identity, their memories, their hopes, dreams, and ambitions for a better life?

How important do you think education and employment is to people living in Direct Provision to enable them to contribute positively to society? To rebuild their lives, to follow their hopes and dreams and to hold on to their own identity while beginning a new life?

Have you thought about the lives refugees had before they had to flee their country? (Education, jobs, homes, community, etc.).

Discussion questions adapted from resource at Teaching ideas Oxfam Education www.oxfam.org.uk/education 'Picturing Food'.

LESSON 10:
MEDIA

Young people are exposed to topical affairs through various media sources every day. It is therefore important that they are media-literate. Teaching media literacy skills works best when combined with activities designed to generate discussion about social and political issues (Vraga & Bode, 2017). In the USA the National Association of Media Literacy Education (NAMLE) defines media literacy as "the ability to access, analyse, evaluate, create and act using all forms of communication". This definition is very useful to apply to GCE, as the ability of a global citizen to be proficient in each of the five domains is relevant to understanding the world and to being an active participant in it.

Hobbs (2021) proposes a theoretical framework for media literacy (**Table 10.1**) This framework is useful to keep in mind when planning for teaching students about media. In addition, there are five key aspects to be aware of when teaching media literacy. All media messages, according to Hobbs (2017):

- Are constructed;
- Are produced within economic, social, political, historical and aesthetic contexts;
- Are interpreted by an interaction between the reader, the text and the culture;
- Use language and other symbol systems associated with different forms and genres of communication;
- Shape people's understanding of and participation in social reality.

In the exercises contained in this lesson, the aim is to develop young people's ability to access, analyse and evaluate media messages.

The initial consideration in teaching media to young people is to concentrate on their media consumption. This includes their sources of information, the news sources they view as reliable and why they view them as such and finally whether young people are capable of assessing their reliability. Marchi (2012) found that young people's main sources of news are trusted adults, social media, blogs and humorous news programmes. Interestingly, it was found that young people often eschew the objective news provided by mainstream organisations and instead prefer to have the information interpreted for them. This seems to suggest that news presented in a convincing, subjective and humorous manner appears more attractive to young people.

Table 10.1: Media Literacy Theoretical Framework

Domains	Concepts	Claims
Authors and Audiences	Author Purpose Audience Usage Interpretations Context Systems	Authors create media messages for different purposes. Authors target specific audiences. People interpret messages in relation to the context in which they experience them and the context in which they were produced. Both authors and audiences add value as part of an economic and political system.
Messages and Meanings	Ideas Emotions Techniques Ideology Effects	Production techniques are used to construct messages. The content of media messages contains values, ideology, and specific points of view. Messages impact people's attitudes and behaviours.
Representation and Realities	Representation Stereotypes Authority Authenticity	Messages are selective representations of reality. Messages use stereotypes to express ideas and information. People judge the credibility of media messages using features like authority and authenticity.

Marchi's (2012) findings were supported by Kahne *et al.* (2012), who noted that family discussions, social media and blogs were strong predictors of online exposure to diverse viewpoints. However, the methods young people used to decide the reliability of the news source differ and many young people incorrectly decide that sites were reliable based on their surface features (Sundar, 2008) or based on its position in search engine results (Hargittai *et al.*, 2010). These concerns about young people's ability to assess reliability were supported by an Ofcom (2018) report on 12 to 15-year-olds media use, which found that a majority of students think critically about which website they use, but only a third understand search engine advertising. Reading and writing skills are vital in critically analysing the media; this is more advantageous to students who are more academically able (Martens & Hobbs, 2015). A further concern is that many young people do not understand humorous videos (Boyer *et al.*, 2015). This inability to distinguish between genuine news and advertising has been exacerbated by the move to viewing media on personal devices rather than shared devices, such as televisions, which has made is harder for parents to help their children understand advertising (Hobbs, 2021). Swart & Broersma (2022) found that young people used pragmatic shortcuts rather than critical analysis for analysing their sources of news. These 'shortcuts' include prior knowledge, cross-referencing, endorsement by friends, family or more distant opinion leaders, familiarity and image of the news brand, perceived risk of the news brand, the institutional character of the news source, the design, tonality and format of the news, and intuition. Worryingly, some of these pragmatic shortcuts have serious shortcomings, such as receiving information from peers which may lead to a false impression of reliability and make people less likely to scrutinise information (Mihailidis & Viotty, 2017).

Guidance

Teaching media literacy requires teachers to encourage students to read online news, comment on current events and, when they find a cause that interests them, connect with relevant online groups and participate in related activities such as volunteering, signing petitions, contacting officials or voting for candidates who support their causes (Boulianne & Theocharis, 2020). A further complication in teaching media is that teachers are often unaware of the benefits of online media. Boyd (2014), for example, notes how digital media can provide more in-depth information. Taking the example of Wikipedia, which is oft derided by teachers as unreliable, she demonstrates how Wikipedia's *'view history'* option can show a diverse range of different arguments and viewpoints behind each entry. In addition, edits must be supported by evidence, available in the *'view source'* option. In contrast, teachers often insist that students seek information from search engines without highlighting how such searches are driven by advertising.

Young people's digital media use is likely to impact their views on many different topical affairs. However, media use that relies solely on areas such as intuition or design, tonality and format has the potential to be abused and ignores the concerns raised relating to advertising, surface features, misunderstanding humorous content and unquestioning acceptance of information received from peers. Moreover, to engage in media literacy education, students must experience a multi-faceted approach and have more engaging aims than simply using it to teach about the reliability of websites or social media posts. Media literacy education should move from analysis of the legitimacy and reliability of websites, to *creating* media and *promoting* the results (Gleason & Von Gillern, 2018; O'Brien, 2021).

Activities

The purpose of the introductory exercise in this lesson is to identify the source of your students' news. We have found that students use a limited amount of news sources and that they primarily engage with social media and conversations with trusted adults, although some may engage with humorous satirical content (though not on a consistent basis). In taking feedback from students, it is important to focus on the *Let's talk about it* section – the idea of different sources for different types of information is important, especially given how young people's news sources are likely to differ from those of adults (for example, some social media platforms such as Facebook and X are viewed as more adult-focused, whereas Snapchat and TikTok are targeted at younger users). A Pew Research Center report (2022) noted that, among the main social media and apps used by US teens, Instagram is probably the only platform where young people and adults share its use. In your questioning, try to focus on the different types of information that different sources facilitate and why that is. Similarly, try to identify the sources of information that students are *not* using and question why that is.

Figure 10.1: US Teens' Use of Social Media/Apps

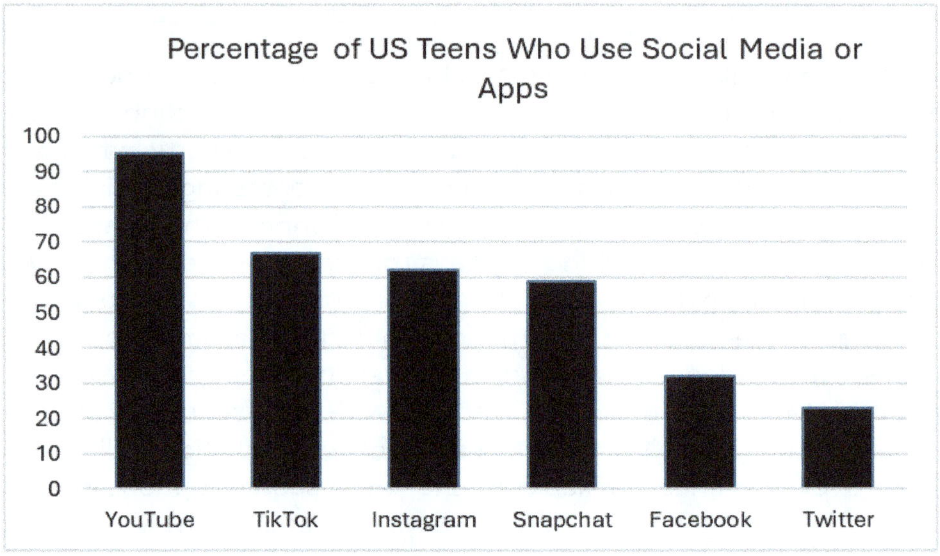

Percentage of US Teens Who Use Social Media or Apps

Platform	Percentage
YouTube	~95
TikTok	~67
Instagram	~62
Snapchat	~59
Facebook	~32
Twitter	~23

Statistics: Pew Research Center (2022).

With 'deepfake' and widespread availability of advanced generative artificial intelligence (AI), the question of altered images becomes more relevant. We found that students are familiar with doctored images and videos on TikTok and other commonly-used social media. Moreover, students frequently engage in altering images and videos. However, these tend to be fun-based and focused on themselves and their friends.

While young people can create fake images and videos, it is equally important for them to be able to identify whether images they view have been modified. The website www.tineye.com provides a means of identifying the origins of pictures that appear online. It allows the user to identify when the photo first appeared online and consequently the original context of the photo. The question of the motivation behind circulating falsified images is often not considered by young people. It is important to examine the purpose behind producing such images. This can be done by questioning why they were produced and identifying the elements in the false image most likely to generate a response. You might focus also on the type of response it aims to generate – emotive, persuasive, amusing or informative or indeed a mixture of all of these. Some altered images can be partisan and spread extensively, such as a widely circulated amended image of former US President Donald Trump wearing what appeared to be soiled white trousers during a game of golf (aimed at giving the impression that Trump was incontinent). In addition, a slowed-down video of former US House of Representatives Speaker, Nancy Pelosi, was disseminated on social media. This video aimed to create the impression that she was inebriated or was suffering from a serious health issue. A satirical video of Leo Varadkar's resignation as Taoiseach (Prime Minister) in Ireland purported to be screened to large crowds who cheered wildly upon this announcement (this image was posted by Little Green on X in 2024). While the purpose was to entertain, the message was nonetheless political.

After considering motivation, look to the consequences of these photos and videos. A constant feature of media attacks on the US President Joe Biden involved editing videos of him speaking to create the impression that he was somehow cognitively impaired. These are referred to as 'cheap fakes' because they simply involve cutting videos or slowing them down (McCarthy, 2022). The motivation was obviously to create the impression that Biden was not capable of doing his job as President. The consequences of such edited media are that it creates the impression, or at least a suspicion, that these videos are genuine (in this case that Biden is unfit for office). Such videos generate much commentary on social media and negative social media comments are more likely to generate an impact (Waddell & Sundar, 2017). Ultimately, these manipulated videos played a part in pressurising President Biden to withdraw from the 2024 Presidential election. As students will be familiar with modified images and videos, it is important to allow them to suggest their own examples as they are more familiar to them.

Finally, you might move from the concept of politics in general to more specific political themes, such as migration. Look at what social media posts show about migration, reference edited photos, videos or photos shown out of context. For example, Donald Trump supporters promoted a photo purporting to show immigrants at the USA-Mexico border. However, the photo was taken in Greece. Likewise, a video of a supposed immigrant stealing a car in Dublin was circulated in 2024 on X by anti-immigration protestors. However, the video was probably made in the UK, without any evidence that the thief was a migrant.

Hobbs (2017) notes that the purpose of media is to inform, persuade and entertain. This also applies to social media. Sometimes all three purposes are intermingled; other times, they exhibit a stand-alone intention. While there are many benefits to social media, it can also act as a driver of polarised behaviour, as people take more and more radical positions to gain attention. We can look here to the media actions of former US President Donald Trump whose posts include untruths, as well as emotively charged and anger-inducing content (Pomerantsev, 2019).

Satirical social media is another media form that can be explored and discussed in class. When doing so, it is essential that students see how satire can interpret others' points of view but exaggerate them to make them seem ridiculous. The US TV show *Saturday Night Live* frequently satirises politicians. One of its most successful examples was its portrayal of former Governor of Alaska Sarah Palin when she was running for the Vice Presidency in the 2008 US general election. A quote from the satirical version of Palin, played by the comedian Tina Fey, claiming that "*I can see Russia from my house*" was based on an interview that Palin did with ABC's Charles Gibson. This misquote has often been attributed to Palin herself. Palin really said, "*They're our next-door neighbours, and you can actually see Russia from land here in Alaska, from an island in Alaska*" (Mikkelson, 2011). The satirical version of Palin helped create the impression that she was not suited to the role of Vice President.

In seeking suitable social media posts and what social issues to examine therein, it might be a good idea to suggest topical issues of relevance (to young people). You might encourage your students to choose information that they come across in their daily lives. Such posts will be more interesting to them.

Common Sense Media (2023) has a checklist for identifying fake news for students that includes the following helpful questions:

- Who created this message?
- Why was the message made?

- Who paid for this message?
- How is the message trying to get your attention?
- Who is represented in the message? Who is missing?

Not all questions apply to every social media post (for instance, there may not be a payment aspect). However, in professionally-produced advertisements, the payment aspect is very relevant. Other factors to question include:

- Is the story hard to believe?
- If so, has it been covered by other papers, websites, channels?
- Does the story come from a poster you've never heard of?
- Does the poster have a reliable reputation?
- Is the story one-sided?
- Are reputable experts quoted?
- Were reliable witnesses mentioned in relation to the article?
- Some partisan news websites have legitimate sounding names. Can you name a few?

It is important for students to realise the distinction between social media and other types of news. Social media contains advantages over other news sources. It is immediate, as people can post information, photos or videos online instantaneously (established organisations must check for veracity and legality). This is especially useful for satisfying people's need for information in cases of emerging stories. However, material posted by people who do not have journalistic training, experience or expertise can lead to untrue, partisan or inaccurate information or, at the very least, information can be posted out of context. A professional journalist working for an established news organisation is more likely to provide an objective report with established facts set in context.

Another consideration in analysing social media posts is the type of information they contain. Sinatra & Lombardi (2020) outline three areas to beware of:

- *Misinformation* occurs when inaccurate information is circulated but without the intent to cause harm;
- *Disinformation*, in contrast, is the intentional spread of false information designed to cause harm;
- *Malinformation* is truthful information that is spread with the express intent of causing harm.

When students are analysing posts, encourage them to beware of and to try to identify these three elements of harmful and misleading content.

In other cases, social media can foster extreme views. Those who promulgate conspiracy theories have access to an immediate audience and, in many cases, their posts can appear to be legitimate and knowledgeable. It is important to help students identify how social media persuades and how posts can be amplified, often falsely, by followers. Instigators of polarising and partisan news on social media often have many followers. However, a significant number of these are fake and create an oft-distorted view of the dominance of certain ideologies (Pomerantsev, 2019).

Sharing information is another consideration in young people's online interactions. We have found that students often share information, photos or videos quickly because they want to be first to have the information. They frequently fail to consider the consequences of sharing this material. Question 4 in this Lesson Plan is based on the foundational idea that young people need to carefully reflect on the information they share. Hobbs (2020) suggests asking students the question "*How might your online sharing affect how other perceive you?*" Looking at how issues such as migration are covered through the lenses of misinformation, disinformation, malinformation, polarised posts and partisan media allows students to explore the checklists mentioned earlier.

In addition to the ability of media forms to persuade and students' ability to assess its reliability, there are other important considerations to critically reflect upon. In the past, consumers were exposed to political, local, sport, legal, entertainment, weather and many different types of news in one programme/paper/magazine. With the advent of online news and websites that have a singular focus, consumers may now only concentrate on the areas that interest them; and many news sources have partisan viewpoints on such news stories. As people get their news from a limited number of sources, they are exposed to only one viewpoint leading to a distorted world view. Many people are unaware of this as they interact in online communities with like-thinking people. Such singular positions influence how people think and may drive some people towards more extreme views. Schkade *et al.* (2007) demonstrated how a homophilic group consensus can cause private positions to become more extreme. In their study, people who had a liberal outlook came together in Boulder to discuss same-sex civil unions, global warming and affirmative action. People with a conservative outlook met to discuss the same topics in Colorado Springs. Prior to meeting, each participant completed an individual questionnaire about their positions on the topics. However, after discussing the topics with like-minded people, the private positions of the participants had become more extreme. Online communities of 'like-thinking' people engaging in common topics (without being exposed to alternative viewpoints) are often referred to as 'echo chambers'. These are frequently compounded by the algorithms used by social media companies that further promote news and viewpoints that people are already interested in (based on stories previously accessed by these people). This phenomenon is referred to as 'filter bubbles' and these are chiefly responsible for creating insulated and polarised communities (Hobbs, 2021). Finally, there is the struggle between directional and accuracy motivation. *Directional motivation* occurs in two cases: when people actively seek out information that confirms their views, this is referred to as *confirmation bias*; and when people reject views that are contrary to their pre-existing ideas, this is referred to as *disconfirmation bias* (Kahne & Bowyer, 2017). *Accuracy motivation*, in contrast means that people will analyse the information more carefully and seek instead to know what is true rather than simply believing something because it is what they want to believe. In teaching media, it is important to promote accuracy motivation. This can be achieved by making people justify opinions, considering different viewpoints and teaching the skill of reflection (Druckman, 2012).

Be aware, therefore, of your class profile before teaching media posts on the topics of migration as some content may embarrass or upset some students. It is also necessary to be vigilant in relation to the tone and content of posts which may be deemed offensive or biased. Another point to emphasise is how information can be taken out of context or manipulated to suit a particular narrative. Rosling *et al.* (2018), for instance, highlight the difficulty Syrians faced fleeing war to seek asylum in Europe. As all EU member states had signed up to the *Geneva Convention*, the Syrians fleeing war would be eligible to seek asylum. However, they could not travel legally to Europe without a visa, causing many to rely on smugglers. The problem was compounded by the EU policy of seizing boats used for people smuggling which led to smugglers instead using flimsy and unsafe boats. This, in turn, led to television images of children who drowned when the boats sank. Consequently, families instead sent their strongest young men on the perilous voyage. Pomerantsev (2019) highlights how all this generated negative media coverage, referring to how so many of the people arriving from Syria were "single men of military age".

In advance of completing this exercise, allocate different media sources to different groups – suggest sites with different outlooks such as *The Guardian*, *The Irish Times*, *The Sun* or *The Daily Mail*. You might use online and print versions, social media and/or suggest satirical programmes and websites – we have found that the more exaggerated the satire, the more engaging it is for students! Posts and responses on X, for example, are available without requiring the students to join or follow posts and the responses are more likely to show examples of echo chambers and partisan responses. Outline clear guidelines on the information that is required for the exercise and ask students not to respond to posts. Explain how hashtags can help them find information on the topic of migration.

Ask the students to complete **Worksheet 10.2** together, then use their responses to guide the ensuing discussion. Taking the answers from groups will help generate a whole class discussion. This can be led by you asking questions such as:

- Does/did every group agree?
- If so, why?
- If not, why not?
- What alternatives would you suggest?

In your questions, focus heavily on the persuasion techniques used to attract and keep attention, such as presenting a view in an oversimplified manner, attacking opponents, taking material out of context, use of humour, etc. Identify whose views are represented and equally whose views are not. In analysing accuracy, focus on the past output of the poster/journalist.

It is important that the students can discover whether evidence has been used to support the claims. If there are examples of evidence, ensure they can evaluate its reliability. You could ask them whether reputable individuals or organisations are used to substantiate claims? If there is no evidence cited, question whether the argument is based on hearsay or urban myths? Sinatra & Lombardi (2020) suggest that when faced with an argument you are unsure of you should ask yourself, "*Is this possible? How do I know?*"

The final exercise is taken from an Economic & Social Research Council (ESRC) funded project called *Digital Wildfire* that ran between 2014 and 2016. The team involved in the project investigated the spread of harmful content on social media such as hate speech, rumours and malicious campaigns and identified opportunities for the responsible governance of digital social spaces.

In this exercise, question why people post offensive content designed to cause hurt. People who engage in such behaviour are referred to as 'trolls'. Ask students to identify how trolling triggers upset. Question the students on the measures that can be taken to prevent posting content designed to cause harm and whether this limits free speech. An example of how irresponsible online behaviour was moderated would be how Twitter began adding warnings to Donald Trump's tweets in the aftermath of his rejection of the results of the 2020 US Presidential election (that they were not relaying accurate information and how he was banned from using the platform in the aftermath of the January 6 riots at Capitol Hill). Interestingly, Angela Merkel, the German Chancellor at the time, criticised the ban for limiting free speech (this case presents as another opportunity for classroom debate).

You may refer to the concept of 'protest' as a means of *taking action*. Investigate the different types of protest students could take part in. In the Katie Hopkins case, students at Brunel University turned their backs on her. Examine other types of protest that could be considered against offensive posts such as blocking people online, responding with facts, posting comments and memes such as '*that never happened*' in response to stories that appear fake. Question the benefits and the disadvantages of each method.

Slacktivism is an uncomplimentary term given to politically active online behaviour, that suggests that digital activism only involves liking a comment, posting a flag or picture beside one's name or signing an online petition. *Saturday Night Live* satirised the concept of slacktivism in the song *Thank you, Scott* (SNL, 2017). However, the word slacktivism may be viewed as pejorative and/or an attempt to demean all types of online political actions; digital activism is a less loaded term (Madison & Klang, 2020). Moreover, many of the criticisms of digital activism are cherrypicked to make it seem as if the actions taken are facile and, in many such cases, the people involved would not consider themselves as activists. In contrast, Madison & Klang (2020) highlight examples of successful digital activism such as during the campaign against the Dakota Access Pipeline when online posts suggested that police were monitoring protestors' Facebook location data. These posts called for people to overwhelm the police's capacity to monitor location data by using Facebook's 'check-in' feature to set their location as Standing Rock. This led to over one million people setting their location at Standing Rock (Torchin, 2016). Examine the concept of digital activism and question when it can be effective and when it may not be effective. Ask your students to give examples of online digital activism they may be aware of or involved with.

Time to Think

In the reflective element of the lesson, it is important to consider the key elements needed to be media-literate. Students should also be able to identify the purpose of media and be able to check its veracity. In relation to the media coverage of migration, consider the language used and why it is used. Pejorative examples include 'unvetted males', 'spongers', 'welfare tourists', 'hoards', 'cultural enhancers' (a term used in a derisive manner by some anti-immigration commentators), while alternative exemplars include 'fellow humans fleeing warzones', 'seeking international protection', etc.

Focus on the students' learning about media in general. Guiding questions could include:

- What did you not know about media that you now understand better?
- What advice would you give to someone when studying media?
- How would you check whether something you came across on media was true or false?
- How has your learning about media impacted how you engage with media?

Focus also on how this understanding of media impacts how migration is covered. From an assessment perspective, question what, if at all, changed over time in relation to students' knowledge, skills, attitudes and values. Ask students to critique media messages and give causal explanations and evidence for such critiques. For instance, the pro-Brexit poster *Breaking Point: The EU Has Failed Us All* was unveiled by Nigel Farage during the Brexit campaign, showing a queue of mostly non-white male migrants. Van Houtom & Bueno Lacy (2017) note that the poster promoted general anxiety, not just about immigration, but especially about asylum seekers from Muslim-majority countries seeking refuge in the EU. Ask students if they can empathise with these effects/affects and if they can identify other media messages that promote a positive or a negative viewpoint on migration. Above all, open up the conversation!

Lesson Plan 10: Media

Purpose of this lesson (learning objectives):
To identify the role of media in influencing opinion

Teacher Materials:
Worksheets 10.1 to 10.3

Format:
- Small group learning
- Whole class learning

	Activity	Let's talk about it
Lead in Where do I get news?	Many young people learn about what is happening from speaking to trusted adults and from satirical political programmes and blog posts (Marchi, 2012). However, many prefer to get information from social media. Ask students where they get their news.	Why are these sources of information trusted by you? Are some sources more appropriate for certain types of information and others for other types of information? What sources would you not consider and why?
Photo of the Ukrainian President's wife	Ask students to look at **Worksheet 10.1**, which purports to show Mrs. Zelenska returning on a private jet having spent lavishly in Paris. A reverse image search on www.TinEye.com showed that the original image had appeared a few months previously when crypto-entrepreneur Richard Heart posted a picture of himself onboard his private plane. The image was manipulated to place Mrs Zelenska's head on his body.	Who do you think may have created such an image? Why do you think this was created? How does it succeed in gaining your attention? Are there any indications that this is not a true photo? Why do you think people might be willing to believe it? Have you encountered similar doctored images that aimed to misrepresent somebody? What was the purpose of this misrepresentation? Have such misrepresentations referred to migration?

	Activity	Let's talk about it

Social media posts	Ask the students to look at social media posts on a range of social issues.
	Remind them to keep in mind that posts that want to persuade will:
	• Aim to activate strong emotions;
	• Oversimplify complex ideas and issues;
	• Attack people with alternative viewpoints;
	• Try to claim the moral high ground.
	Working in pairs. Ask students to identify three posts where these features apply.
	• What is the purpose of the post?
	• What factors are employed to convince others?
	• Is the poster reliable:
	   o Does he/she have any experience/qualification in the area?
	   o Is he/she promoting something that you have not come across anywhere else?
	   o Is he/she referring to reliable evidence to support his/her ideas?
	   o Who are his/her followers?
	   o Why is this person posting this information?
		When can social media be useful for gaining information?
		What are the risks of gaining your information from social media? Why is this?
		Do you believe people can be influenced by people with bad intentions on social media? Why/why not?
		Would you share any of the posts you looked at? Why/why not?

Questions to ask about the media	Ask the students to find an example of how migration is covered in the media, across a range of different types of sources – television, online, newspapers, satirical programmes, social media posts. Then ask the students to complete **Worksheet 10.2** and to evaluate the reliability of the media example chosen.	Was there a difference in the representation of migration over different media types? Which types had greater reference to evidence and expert opinion? Who was missing from the representations? Why do you think there is such a difference in representing the issue across different media types? What have you learned about how issues are represented in media?
Katie Hopkins – 'Professional Troll'	Read **Worksheet 10.3** and answer the questions in small groups. Take feedback by asking each group's response to each question. Invite other groups to suggest alternative responses they gave to the questions.	Can you think of other people who make social media posts that cause offence to others? Why do they do it? What has been the response of others?

Time to think
What have you learned about how the media can represent topics? How can this impact views on migration?

Worksheet 10.1: Mrs. Zelenska

Source: https://www-media.aap.co.au/wp-content/uploads/2022/12/22141143/ukraine.jpg.

Worksheet 10.2: Questioning the Media

Select a media report, column, post, etc., dealing with the issue of migration and complete the worksheet below.

Title of the Media Example	
What type of media is it?	
Who created this message?	
Why was the message created?	
Is its message aiming to inform, persuade or entertain?	
What is the message's intended audience?	
Who paid for the message? What else have they paid for?	
What techniques are used to get your attention?	
What techniques are used to keep your attention?	
Whose points of views and values are represented in this message?	
Whose points of views and values are missing?	
Are there examples of intolerant language used?	
Has evidence been used to support the arguments?	
Have experts been quoted? If they are referred to as experts, do you think they are genuine experts?	
How reliable is this media example? Explain your decision.	

Based on *Five Questions to Ask About the Media* www.commonsense.org/education.

Worksheet 10.3: Katie Hopkins – 'Professional Troll'

Katie Hopkins is a broadcaster and businesswoman. She became a celebrity after competing in *The Apprentice* and now has her own newspaper columns and appears regularly on television programmes. She has over 600,000 followers on Twitter/X and is known for posting very provocative opinions on the platform. These often cause offence as well as heated debate. She has been reported to the police for posting apparently hateful comments about immigrants. She has posted tweets criticising fat people, people with tattoos, parents who name their children after geographic locations, and people with ginger hair.

Hopkins has been described as 'the most hated woman in Britain' and a 'professional troll'. Petitions have been set up to demand her removal from social media, but many people express agreement with her views.

In November 2015, Hopkins went to Brunel University to join a debate. As she started to speak, around 50 students in the audience stood up and turned their backs to her before walking out of the room. This was a planned act of protest against her inclusion in the debate. Afterwards Hopkins described the protestors as a 'generation raised on social media' who have been taught 'what to think not how to think'.

Further information

- http://www.express.co.uk/news/uk/596385/Katie-Hopkins-Apprentice-racism-quiz-police-migrants
- http://www.dailymail.co.uk/news/article-3247431/MailOnline-hires-outspoken-TV-personality-Katie-Hopkins-columnist.html
- http://www.standard.co.uk/showbiz/celebrity-news/katie-hopkins-slams-a-generation-of-students-raised-on-social-media-after-brunel-university-walkout-a3124376.html

Points for discussion

Why do some people get upset about what Katie Hopkins posts on social media?

What makes someone a professional troll? Do you think Katie Hopkins can be described as a professional troll?

Do you think Katie Hopkins should be banned from social media?

Why did the students at Brunel turn their backs on Katie Hopkins? Do you think this was an effective form of protest? What other things can people do if they don't like someone's comments on social media?

Do you agree with what Katie Hopkins said about the students at Brunel?

Extracted from the Digital Wildfire Project – www.digitalwildfire.org

DEVELOPING AS A GLOBAL CITIZENSHIP EDUCATOR THROUGH REFLECTIVE PRACTICE

In the **Introduction** to this book, as well as in **Lesson 1**, we critically engaged with what Global Citizenship Education (GCE) is all about. The 10 lessons provided exemplars of how GCE can be taught and learned effectively. In this final section, we focus on the importance of reflective practice – how you might think about GCE and how you can identify key disciplinary features that positively impact your teaching. Becoming a teacher of GCE can be challenging, as teachers often feel they lack the required knowledge, pedagogical skills and training. However, we suggest that, first and foremost, amongst the prerequisites for good GCE teaching is a willingness to engage with global issues with an open and enquiring mind. Moreover, in your genuine attempts to nurture good global citizenry, you are already demonstrating a good understanding of the discipline and modelling its key principles and aims.

Thus, Guo (2014, p.2) says that a global citizen should demonstrate some or all the following characteristics:

- Respecting fellow humans, regardless of race, gender, age, religion, or political views;
- Appreciating diversity and multiple perspectives;
- Holding a view that no single society or culture is inherently superior to any other;
- Cherishing the natural world and respecting the rights of all living things;
- Practising and encouraging sustainable patterns of living, consumption and production;
- Striving to resolve conflicts without the use of violence;
- Being responsible for solving pressing global challenges in whichever way one can;
- Thinking globally and acting locally in eradicating inequality and injustice in all their forms.

In this chapter, we focus on how you can progress your journey as a GCE educator. Your personal/professional development focuses on:

- The knowledge, skills, attitudes and values you bring to, and gain from, GCE;
- The use you make of worldly (oft feared as 'controversial') issues in your lessons;
- The impact of your own changing identity on teaching GCE;

- How you effectively – and more expansively – assess your students' learning; and
- How you continually reflect on your GCE teaching trajectory.

Becoming a Globally Competent Teacher

The key learning outcomes of GCE, as outlined by UNESCO (2015, p. 22), relate to each of the core conceptual dimensions of GCE, as listed below.

Table 11.1: Learning Outcomes for GCE

Cognitive
Learners: • Acquire knowledge and understanding of local, national and global issues and the interconnectedness and interdependency of different countries and populations. • Develop skills for critical thinking and analysis.
Socio-emotional
Learners: • Experience a sense of belonging to a common humanity, sharing values and responsibilities, based on human rights. • Develop attitudes of empathy, solidarity and respect for differences and diversity.
Behavioural
Learners: • Act effectively and responsibly at local, national and global levels for a more peaceful and sustainable world. • Develop motivation and willingness to take necessary actions.

To teach GCE effectively, then, a teacher must aim to achieve these worthy outcomes. In attempting to do so, the teacher seeks to:

- Understand the rationale for GCE philosophy;
- Develop a capacity to plan lessons that allow these outcomes to be achieved;
- Evaluate their students' learning;
- Demonstrate to their students how to take some action whenever they encounter injustice.

In essence, these elements require the teacher to become 'globally competent' which, according to Guo (2014, p. 4) entails four key competences:

- Knowledge of the interdependency of world events and issues;
- Pedagogical skills to help students analyse and appreciate multiple perspectives and multicultural traditions;
- Intercultural competency and greater adaptability to the range of social and cultural norms that are faced in their classrooms; and
- Commitment to assist students in becoming responsible global citizens.

These competences are closely linked to the core GCE knowledge, skills, attitudes and values that we hope to have demonstrated in this *Handbook*. Practically, we suggest that you might focus on developing your practice in those areas.

Knowledge

Consider the knowledge you need to acquire to teach GCE topics. Additionally, consider how you will gain this knowledge. We suggest that multiple opportunities exist such as reading widely, keeping abreast of news and current affairs, sourcing relevant documentaries, listening to first-hand witness accounts, observing how issues are represented on social media, becoming aware of, and accepting, the challenges linked to cultural differences and examining these sources of information with an analytical mind. You might evaluate different viewpoints, rather than just accepting your own. As you develop your knowledge base, you will become more aware of how different actions and events are linked. This knowledge bank will provide more detailed understandings and will serve as useful material to share with your students to enable them also to better understand GCE-related issues. This process of developing knowledge is on-going – it is in a state of constant flux, as 'facts' and policies change, and as events occur.

We use the following example to demonstrate how exposure to factual information can develop one's knowledge by looking at two writers on the issue of migration. Thus, Collier (2013) shows how increased migration leads to an increased diaspora developing within host countries. As this diaspora increases in size it leads, according to Collier (*ibid.*), to reduced interaction between immigrants and the indigenous population; to a widening cultural distance and reduced trust between both groups. These factors push governments to make reactionary decisions (the 'panic phase') on migration policies. Collier (*ibid.*) contends that migration policies should consider immigrants, and he includes here those people left behind in the countries of origin, as well as the host population. However, policies created in the 'panic phase' or the subsequent 'ugly' phase are reactionary and are aimed only at satisfying disquiet amongst the more vocal elements of the indigenous population – they do not consider the best interests of every group. An example of the repercussions of one policy made in the panic phase is outlined by another writer, Hayden (2022), who looks at the human impact of the migration policies put in place by the European Union (EU) to prevent migrants crossing the Mediterranean Sea. The EU provided financial support to the Libyan Coastguard to prevent migrants attempting to escape from Libya and to return them to Libyan detention centres. Here, many became enslaved, and their families were blackmailed into sending money for their release. Both writers make important contributions to the topic of migration, both sources are fact-based, and both look at a complicated issue from different (in this case, economic and social/human rights) perspectives. Such information nurtures our collective knowledge and enables students to critically analyse the causes and consequences of migration policies, for example.

Skills

View the development of skills as a two-fold process: Consider, firstly, the skills you want your students to develop through GCE, but also the skills you need to acquire to achieve this. GCE allows learners to develop the skills of critical inquiry, media literacy and an understanding of how information is mediated and communicated (UNESCO, 2015, p.23).

We suggest that you engage in discussions on topics you plan to use in GCE lessons. This allows you to examine your ability to enable students to respectfully express opinions on topics and it develops your capacity to respond to alternative viewpoints. Additionally, you may need to acquire new pedagogical skills to enable students to question the world around them. By using simple didactic, direct instructional methods, the notion of a 'right and wrong' view is (unwittingly) promoted and there is little room for contextual learning. While students may accept a 'correct' response dictated by you, they are equally likely to be swayed by convincing counter viewpoints. By promoting the skills of critical discussion, debate and deliberation, students learn to more genuinely engage with the topic, to form their own opinions based on evidence, to learn how to scientifically defend these opinions.

The skills involved in information retrieval and research are key here. Simply regurgitating other people's arguments, even when you may agree with them, and without teaching students how to evaluate these arguments or examine the evidence behind their claims, ultimately fails to develop their knowledge and skills. GCE skills include being taught how to research, make presentations, marshal arguments, discuss topics, give alternative opinions in a non-confrontational manner, to raise concerns with people in positions of power and how to take action. We suggest that you identify the skills you need to teach GCE, consider how to develop them and use them demonstrably with your students. If students do not see these skills modelled by you, they are unlikely to develop them for and with themselves.

We recommend conducting an audit of the knowledge you already have before teaching a topic, then try to identify the knowledge you need. Equally, you could conduct an audit on the skills you currently have and those you may require. Then note how you plan to achieve these. A template is suggested in **Table 11.2**.

Attitudes

Attitudes are specific judgements about anything (or anyone) that can be evaluated (Hanel *et al.*, 2021). Essentially, they are a person's likes or dislikes. Attitudes can be positive or negative, vary in their strength and in their view of whether something is moral or immoral.

Prior to teaching a topic, we suggest that you consider your own attitudes to the topic and, once you have identified them, question why you hold these attitudes, whether they are informed by evidence and/or emotion, as well as how they link with your values (see below). Consider in planning your lessons how these attitudes are actually central to your GCE work and begin to explore ideal attitudes that you wish the students to develop. It is important to decide whether you will share your attitudes with your students and, if you do decide to share them, to ask yourself "Why?" Conversely, if you opt not to share your attitudes with your students, ask yourself "Why not?"

Table 11.2: Audit of Knowledge & Skills Required to Teach a Topic

TOPIC		
Knowledge		
Knowledge (including materials, information, etc.) I already have to teach this topic.	Knowledge I need to gain to teach this topic effectively.	How will I gain this knowledge?
Skills		
Skills I already have to teach this topic.	Skills I need to gain to teach this topic effectively.	How will I develop these skills?

We suggest that developing attitudes that promote inclusion and tolerance to diverse viewpoints and people, as well as attitudes that have been formed by questioning other people's stances, are essential features of good GCE teaching. Attitudes inevitably play a major role, because they provide a means of demonstrating our values. For example, a person who holds positive attitudes towards cycling and who buys products locally is likely also to be somebody who values and cares for the environment (Hanel *et al.*, 2021).

Values

Values may be considered as generally positive, abstract and trans-situational guiding principles in our lives that impact our feelings towards objects or people and thereby influence our behaviour (Hanel *et al.*, 2021). Schwartz (2012) identified 10 basic human values that are common across cultures. However, there are considerable differences in how individuals and groups prioritise these values because people instantiate (or understand) these values differently (Hanel *et al.*, 2021). Some values, such as benevolence and power, may conflict with each other while other values, such as conformity and security, are more compatible. Schwartz grouped these 10 values into four higher-order groups: openness to change; conservation values; self-transcendence; and self-enhancement. Values in the 'openness to change' group contrast with values in the 'conservation' group. Similarly, values in the 'self-transcendence' group contrast with values in the 'self-enhancement' category. **Table 11.3** below outlines the 10 values and briefly defines them, while **Figure 11.1** places them within the higher-order groups.

Because our values influence our attitudes and our behaviour, it is important both to identify them and to know how we instantiate them. The global citizenship educator's values ought to include 'openness to change' and 'self-transcendence' to assist students becoming responsible citizens.

Table 11.3: Schwartz's Basic Values (2012)

Value	Definition
Self-direction	Independent thought and action – choosing, creating, exploring.
Stimulation	Excitement, novelty, and challenge in life.
Hedonism	Pleasure or sensuous gratification for oneself.
Achievement	Personal success through demonstrating competence according to social standards.
Power	Social status and prestige, control or dominance over people and resources.
Security	Safety, harmony, and stability of society, of relationships, and of self.
Conformity	Restraint of actions, inclinations, and impulses likely to upset or harm others and violate social expectations or norms. Conformity entails subordination to persons with whom one frequently interacts - parents, teachers, and bosses.
Tradition	Respect, commitment, and acceptance of the customs and ideas that one's culture or religion provides. Tradition entails subordination to abstract objects – religious and cultural customs and ideas.
Benevolence	Preserving and enhancing the welfare of those with whom one is in frequent personal contact.
Universalism	Understanding, appreciation, tolerance, and protection for the welfare of all people and for nature.

Figure 11.1: Schwartz's Theoretical Model of Relations among 10 Motivational Types of Value (2012)

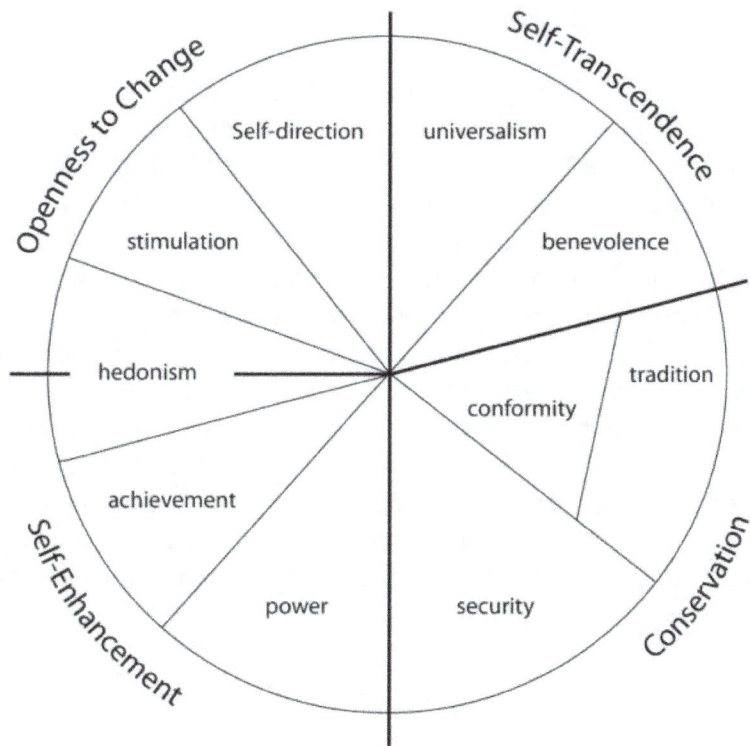

Of course, values can be difficult to identify and measure. However, an important consideration in GCE is highlighting similarities and differences in values between groups, as this helps to demonstrate that there are more similarities and less differences between us. Moreover, emphasising similarities helps to reduce prejudice and prioritise our shared goals (Hanel *et al.*, 2021).

It is important to recognise that there is no defined (or definitive) level of knowledge, list of skills, correct attitudes or set of values that are required to become a competent GCE educator. That said, having an awareness and understanding of each of these areas (including their constantly changing nature), as well as demonstrating the will and capacity to develop them through reflective practice, are all essential characteristics needed for nurturing one's global competence.

'Controversial' Issues

GCE challenges existing beliefs and mindsets and focuses on addressing wrongs in society and in the world. Consequently, teaching certain worldly issues or points of view has the potential to be 'controversial'. Controversial issues may be defined as:

... questions of public policy that spark significant disagreement. These are authentic questions about the kinds of public policies that should be adopted to address public problems – they are not hypothetical. Such issues require deliberation among a 'we' to determine which policy is the best response to a particular problem. (Hess, 2009, p.37)

or:

... ones where the best answer has yet to be determined to the satisfaction of the majority of informed persons. (Zimmerman & Robertson, 2017, p.48)

Schools are suitable places for discussing such topics. Here, there are curricular opportunities to discuss worldly issues and teachers are, and can become, skilful in teaching students how to participate in topical discussions. Schools provide crucial opportunities for students to hear opinions that differ from their own (Hess, 2009, p.22). Discussing so-called 'controversial' issues helps students develop the skills to construct and evaluate arguments which, in turn, enables them to be more open to alternative viewpoints and advance the key skill of deliberation (Zimmerman & Robertson, 2017). The capacity to develop insights and viewpoints, based on facts and evidence, is a key consideration in GCE and demonstrates how emergent knowledge and skills, combined with renewed attitudes and values, form an important foundation for students' learning. Exposure to 'controversial' topics reveals the existence of different opinions, how each can have value (when supported by evidence) and how they depend on context. These factors are underlined by Hannah Arendt (1968, p.238):

> **... facts inform opinions, and opinions, inspired by different interests and passions, can differ widely and still be legitimate as long as they respect factual truth. Freedom of opinion is a farce unless factual information is guaranteed and the facts themselves are not in dispute.**

Discussing controversial issues also allows students to consider the viewpoint of the person not being represented (Arendt, 1968, p.241):

> **I form an opinion by considering a given issue from different viewpoints, by making present to my mind the standpoints of those who are absent; that is I represent them... the more people's standpoints I have present in my mind while I am pondering a given issue, and the better I can imagine how I would feel and think if I were in their place, the stronger will be my capacity for representative thinking and the more valid my final conclusions, my opinion.**

Without exposure to alternative positions, people will form opinions based only on their own social group context and self-interest (Arendt, 1968, p.242):

> **... of course I can refuse to do this and form an opinion that takes only my own interests, or the interests of the group to which I belong, into account; nothing indeed is more common, even among highly sophisticated people, than blind obstinacy that becomes manifest in lack of imagination and failure to judge.**

Many topics present as either open or closed. An 'open topic' is one where there are a range of different opinions, and no definite answer, whereas a 'closed topic' is one that has been decided upon, such as women's suffrage (Hess, 2009). Some topics are 'tipping' – this means they are moving from 'open to closed' or indeed 'closed to open' and, because they are 'tipping', there are people who support the 'tip' and others who don't (*ibid*.). Therefore, this renders certain topics as 'controversial' (*ibid*.).

There are, however, valid reasons why teachers eschew such topics, including:

- **Pedagogical reasons:** Teachers may believe that classroom deliberation does not reflect the political world, the teacher may feel unprepared to teach the subject matter, or the curriculum is already seen as too crowded to consider any further challenges (Zimmerman & Robertson, 2017);
- **Parental concerns:** Some parents view schools as places for preparing their children for further education and not for discussing political or social issues (Hess, 2009), or some religious parents may object to the idea that something they believe in is presented as being open for discussion (Zimmerman & Robertson, 2017);
- **Contested views of citizenship:** There is a wide range of views as to what is meant by citizenship. Westheimer & Kahne (2004) outline three citizen types, with most citizenship education programmes falling into one of these – the 'personally responsible', 'participatory' and 'justice-oriented'. The 'personally responsible' citizen simply lives a good life and obeys rules; the 'participatory citizen' organises responses to challenges in society, such as fundraisers; while the 'justice-oriented citizen' questions the sources of inequalities and problems in society and

pushes to address these. The second and third models come closer to meeting the learning outcomes of GCE, as outlined previously by UNESCO (2015). However, school management, parents, students and teachers often view the first model as that most suited to education. Challenging this assumption can be difficult.

In addressing these challenges to discussion, debate or deliberative activities, it is important to consider why you want to introduce the issue, what you want the students to learn, the potential negative repercussions and challenges you may face, and how you plan to overcome them. Hess (2009) says that the elements students look for in classroom discussion include:

- The opportunity to problem-solve by engaging in discussion about complex grown-up issues;
- The respect of their teacher – while the expression of a particular point of view by a teacher is important, it may, if it is too forceful, prevent the students offering a counter opinion;
- Fair play – the right to share opinions without the teacher taking over the discussion.

Consider how to plan discussions that include these three elements. We recommend setting ground rules prior to conducting the discussion that outline how you plan to operate the discussion. When planning discussions, you may be reticent to broach certain topics because of the profile of students in your class. Consider how other scenarios with similar consequences or messages could be covered without directly impacting students in your class. For instance, in the case of a student who may have been directly impacted by an ongoing conflict, you could instead look to how a similar conflict may have impacted people elsewhere. In this respect, you are not presenting yourself as an expert and you are not focusing on an experience that somebody in the class may have directly experienced. This approach also enables the students to find their own space to contribute, but only if they want to do so. 'Controversial' issues, by their nature, are challenging, but many problems can be pre-empted or can be learned through experience. How you will discuss these topics in future lessons can always be improved upon!

Teacher Identity

A teacher's identity is likely to impact on how they approach GCE. Identity is continuously forming due to the influence of internal factors, such as personality characteristics, special abilities or talents (Pennington & Richards, 2016), as well as external factors like one's job context and life experiences (Beauchamp & Thomas, 2009), and one's socio-economic status, societal position and/or connection to social groups (Pennington & Richards, 2016). In addition to matters traditionally associated with 'self', a teacher's identity encompasses such areas as subject knowledge, pedagogical and didactical knowledge (Beauchamp & Thomas, 2009). Identity also encompasses the situated context of activities, such as the teacher-in-the-classroom, colleague-in-the-staffroom, the partner- or parent-in-the-home (Pennington & Richards, 2016). Finally, a person's self-image and self-awareness are often based on certain values and beliefs about how people should behave towards others (Pennington & Richards, 2016).

Within the classroom, for example, the teacher's identity reflects the teacher's own view of what being a teacher entails; but it will also reflect their life experiences, the student population, the subject being taught, the content of instruction and/or the school cultural context. Classroom identity may see the teacher self-promote a detached and formal teacher identity for reasons to do with classroom management, school expectations, parental expectations, policies and/or other requirements (Pennington & Richards, 2016). However, such changes to the teacher's identity are a normal part of identity development and often occur in response to curricular, assessment and/or other contextual factors (Pennington & Richards, 2016). We suggest that the type of identity you can adopt in the GCE classroom may differ from your view of your traditional teaching role. In the previous section, for instance, we looked at discussing 'controversial' issues. To do this work may necessitate a move away from traditional, directional approaches which could undermine the whole concept of enabling students to think for themselves.

Reflection – as per the focus of this final section of the *Handbook* – provides a key means for teachers to shape their own identity (Beauchamp & Thomas, 2009). Teachers who are aware of their life experiences can use these experiences to develop their practice. We have witnessed – through Teacher Education programmes – how student teachers' backgrounds outside the classroom have helped them create very engaging and informed lessons. The knowledge and insights gained from working on a co-operative farm in Central America or working as an extreme sports coach in Africa, for example, further enables student teachers to teach creative, informed and enjoyable lessons. However, many teachers will not have considered elements of their identity that can bring their lessons to life in the classroom. There tends to be a catalyst, a reason why teachers opt to specifically teach GCE and why they see its value. It may stem from a single episode that influenced them profoundly or it may be due to the way that they live on an on-going basis. Many teachers will have lived in different cultures, allowing them to draw on these experiences; other teachers will have worked in different professions, or have been involved in volunteer work. Certainly, people who are more aware of their identity can develop their own sense of agency (Beauchamp & Thomas, 2009). Increased awareness of your identity will, we suggest, give you confidence and will empower you to develop your own capacity as a GCE teacher.

It is important to interrogate all your attitudes and actions that are linked to your identity and that may influence your teaching. It is true that, while some areas of your identity may develop your teaching of GCE, others may limit it. When considering your teacher identity in GCE then, there are many different factors involved. Contextual factors such as school gender (O'Brien, 2023b; Tormey & Gleeson, 2012), socio-economic status of the students and their families (Goren & Yemini, 2017; O'Brien, 2023c; Wood, 2014), the nature of the learner population, the impact of colleagues and school administrators, as well as teaching discipline (Beauchamp & Thomas, 2009), all have a bearing. Consider too personal elements of identity – gender appears to have little bearing, with only minor differences found between male and female teachers (O'Brien, 2023d; Sansone, 2017), whereas other areas, such as migrant status, are significant factors. Kim (2021), for example, showed how migrant teachers de-emphasise national and white-focused notions of citizenship and use their own life experiences to validate and incorporate their students' diverse cultural backgrounds in teaching citizenship. A myriad of other factors may also impact how GCE is taught, such as one's family circumstances, sexuality and/or religion.

Rosling (Rosling *et al.*, 2018, p.182) recounts the reaction of the Chairperson of the African Union Commission, Nkosazana Dlamini-Zuma, to a speech he made about reducing extreme poverty in Africa:

> **As a finishing remark, you said that you hoped your grandchildren would come as tourists to Africa and travel on the new high-speed trains we plan to build. What kind of vision is that? It is the same old European vision. It is my grandchildren who are going to visit your continent and travel on your high-speed trains and visit the exotic ice hotel I've heard you have in northern Sweden. It is going to take a long time, we know that. It is going to take lots of wise decisions and large investments. But my 50-year vision is that Africans will be welcome tourists in Europe and not unwanted refugees.**

On reflecting on this interaction, Rosling realised that his identity as a European middle-class man impacted how he viewed Africa. We suggest that you might now consider the elements of your own background and your teacher professional identity that you emphasise and reflect on how you think they impact your teaching. This can include consideration of the subject matter you study and teach, the skills you employ, your attitudes towards the people or situations being engaged in and, above all, your own values.

In a practical sense, you could consider the following question prompts:

- What topics do you prioritise?
- Do you tend to promote discussion or dictate information?
- Does the attitude of school management or parents towards GCE impact how you teach it?
- Is your classroom layout suited to discussion or direct instruction?
- What do the walls of your classroom look like?
- Do students pick their seats, or do you assign them?
- What factors in your personal story impact your teaching in GCE?

Assessment

UNESCO (2015, p.56) outlines four questions to consider when deciding how to assess GCE programmes:

- What are the core areas of learning to be addressed in a comprehensive assessment and evaluation plan?
- How will we know if learners are successfully learning? What indicators can be used?
- What will we accept as evidence of learners' understanding and skill development?
- What types of assessment will be most useful to collect evidence of learning?

Teachers are constantly assessing their students. In-class assessment includes recognising the students' level of interest or enthusiasm, their ability to conduct tasks, discuss or simply ask questions. Over the course of Junior Cycle education, students have gained experience of varying classroom-based assessments, such as presentations, fact-finding projects and drawing up reports. Consequently, teachers and students will already have experience of devising methods of assessment that involve creating knowledge, developing skills and promoting positive attitudes and values. We believe the methods of assessment you choose to evaluate your students' learning in GCE will vary depending on several factors including your own preferred assessment methods, the students, the school context, the material covered, and the skills involved in specific learning activities. However, we can make some suggestions that may be useful to you.

Hess (2009, p.73), for example, outlines a method for scoring discussions (**Table 11.4**). We think that this is a wonderful, creative exemplar to use – it provides a very useful rubric to assess students' discussions and, because it awards points, it can teach students how to conduct discussions in a more productive manner.

Table 11.4: Bob Martin's Scoring Checklist for Scored Discussions

Positive	Negative
1. Making a relevant comment (+ 1) 2. Using probing questions to elicit more information or to get someone involved in the discussion (+ 1) 3. Using evidence to support a statement (+ 1) 4. Challenging the relevancy of a person's comment or use of evidence (+ 2) 5. Using evidence from personally gathered sources to support a statement (+ 2) 6. Summarising the discussion (+ 2) 7. Recognising a contradiction in someone's opinion (+ 2) 8. Making a stipulation (+ 2) 9. Making a concession (+ 2) 10. Making a clear transition to a relevant issue (+ 3) 11. Identifying and explaining a value conflict (+ 3) 12. Stating and explaining an appropriate analogy (+ 3)	1. Making an irrelevant comment (– 1) 2. Not paying attention (– 1) 3. Interrupting another discussant to prevent them from participating (– 2) 4. Lack of or inappropriate evidence when making a factual statement (– 2) 5. Monopolising/dominating a discussion to prevent others from participating (– 3) 6. Making a personal attack (– 4)
Additional Notes Individually, students may not receive more than 18 points per discussion. An additional 1 to 5 points are added to each individual's score on the basis of the overall discussion's quality, for a maximum of 23 points. A maximum of 3 points may be earned on positive comment 1 and a maximum of 8 points may be earned between positive comments 3 and 5.	

Prowse & Forsyth (2018) state that assessment in GCE must demonstrate that students have developed their knowledge, skills, values and attributes and that they can finally articulate their learning. They suggest that different subject disciplines could assess different aspects of GCE – economic elements of GCE, for instance, could be assessed within the remit of business-related subjects, whereas the moral aspect of GCE could be assessed within the remit of the humanities. We would add that a teacher's subject discipline is likely to be of benefit here – for instance, a science teacher could use an assessment such as analysing the environmental impact of a proposal, or a mathematics teacher could ask students to cost a financial plan to develop a community facility.

Assessing students' values is a more complicated task. Prowse & Forsyth (2018) propose that Schwartz's Values Survey or Portrait Values Questionnaire could be used to measure the relative importance of the 10 values outlined by Schwartz (referenced earlier in this chapter). We suggest the short version of the Portrait Values Questionnaire (Schwartz, 2003), added in the **Appendix** to this chapter, which could be used to assess values development. **Table 11.5** below shows how each question is related to a value from Schwartz's Basic Values. Values in the 'self-transcendence' and 'openness to change' areas appear most suited to GCE work (Prowse & Forsyth, 2018).

Table 11.5: Schwartz's 21 Item Portrait Values Questionnaire (2003, pp.311-312)

G1	Thinking up new ideas and being creative is important to him [sic.]. He likes to do things in his [sic.] own original way.	Self-direction (Openness to change)
G2	It is important to him to be rich. He wants to have a lot of money and expensive things.	Power (Self-enhancement)
G3	He thinks it is important that every person in the world should be treated equally. He believes everyone should have equal opportunities in life.	Universalism (Self-transcendence)
G4	It's important to him to show his abilities. He wants people to admire what he does.	Achievement (Self-enhancement)
G5	It is important to him to live in secure surroundings. He avoids anything that might endanger his safety.	Security (Conservation)
G6	He likes surprises and is always looking for new things to do. He thinks it is important to do lots of different things in life.	Stimulation (Openness to change)
G7	He believes that people should do what they are told. He thinks people should follow rules at all times, even when no-one is watching.	Conformity (Conservation)
G8	It is important to him to listen to people who are different from him. Even when he disagrees with them, he still wants to understand them.	Universalism (Self-transcendence)
G9	It is important to him to be humble and modest. He tries not to draw attention to himself.	Tradition (Conservation)
G10	Having a good time is important to him. He likes to "spoil" himself.	Hedonism (Openness to change/self-enhancement)
G11	It is important to him to make his own decisions about what he does. He likes to be free and not depend on others.	Self-direction (Openness to change)
G12	It's very important to him to help the people around him. He wants to care for their well-being.	Benevolence (Self-transcendence)

G13	Being very successful is important to him. He hopes people will recognise his achievements.	Achievement (Self-enhancement)
G14	It is important to him that the government ensures his safety against all threats. He wants the state to be strong so it can defend its citizens.	Security (Conservation)
G15	He looks for adventures and likes to take risks. He wants to have an exciting life.	Stimulation (Openness to change)
G16	It is important to him always to behave properly. He wants to avoid doing anything people would say is wrong.	Conformity (Conservation)
G17	It is important to him to get respect from others. He wants people to do what he says.	Power (Self-enhancement)
G18	It is important to him to be loyal to his friends. He wants to devote himself to people close to him.	Benevolence (Self-transcendence)
G19	He strongly believes that people should care for nature. Looking after the environment is important to him.	Universalism (Self-transcendence)
G20	Tradition is important to him. He tries to follow the customs handed down by his religion or his family.	Tradition (Conservation)
G21	He seeks every chance he can to have fun. It is important to him to do things that give him pleasure.	Hedonism (Openness to change/self-enhancement)

We do not see these suggestions as the sole means of assessing your students' learning, but they can be part of a range of different assessments that you employ. Prowse & Forsyth (2018, pp.616-617) outline a series of questions to guide assessment design in GCE that we include below. We suggest that you do not need to respond to each question but, together with the UNESCO (2015) assessment questions, they allow you to consider the fundamental elements of any GCE assessment:

- Does the task take account of the diverse experiences and attributes students bring to it and allow them to integrate these into their submission?
- Will students feel motivated to perform the task well?
- Will I enjoy assessing the students' work?
- Will students feel able to self- and peer-assess their work?
- Will the assessment process be manageable for this task?
- Could an assessor self-assess against these assessment related questions?
    - What aspects of GCE are being assessed?
    - How will students show their achievement of outcomes or attributes?
    - How explicit are the GCE aspects of the assignment in the information provided?
    - Can students see how they will develop as global citizens?
    - Is the information transparent and how is this checked?
    - Is the information accessible to all students?
    - How explicit are the GCE aspects of the assignment in your teaching?

- Do you use examples which demonstrate the values you associate with GCE?
- Do you encourage critique of GCE?
- Are submissions arrangements accessible to all (for example, facilitating commuting students, those with disabilities, carers, those who celebrate religious holidays)?
- Do marking schemes capture your GCE intentions (for example, integrating a discussion of values or a development of attributes)?
- Is feedback linked to future development? Does it specifically mention GCE attributes?
- After completion of the assignments, do you feel that students moved forward as global citizens? Do they know this?
- What stands out in terms of students' development as global citizens?
- What might enhance the integration of GCE in this assignment next time?

There are many ways of assessing students' learning in GCE. We do not provide a set assessment because we recognise that the context in which you are conducting GCE may differ – the time allocation, whether GCE is taught within subjects or as a stand-alone module, your learner profile and school assessment practices will all impact the assessment most suitable to you. However, we hope that by highlighting different areas and methods of assessment, and by providing different question prompts, this may benefit you in assessing the knowledge, skills, attitudes and values of your own students.

Reflection

Having considered the areas we have referenced in this chapter, we suggest that you might begin a process of self-reflection. As has been argued, reflection is a key means of enhancing your professional practice. It examines what you do and why you do it and it is ultimately aimed at self-improvement. There are many different models of reflection on teaching 'out there'. One commonly used model is that of Gibbs' Reflection Cycle (1988). We feel that this is a particularly good example of a user-friendly model that considers the teacher's feelings and includes action points that are linked to reflective groundings. The circular nature of reflection is itself signalled and the model outlines six different stages of the reflective process:

- **Description:** The teacher simply describes what happened in the lesson;
- **Feelings:** The teacher identifies the feelings they felt at the time, but also the feelings that they now have when looking back;
- **Evaluation:** The teacher evaluates what went well and what did not go well in the lesson. Factors to consider would be students' reactions, the teacher's comfort or discomfort, etc. At this stage, the teacher makes value judgments;
- **Analysis:** The teacher tries to make sense of the situation. Greater thought is given to the factors that helped or impeded the lesson. Considerations at this stage include looking at ideas from outside the experience and looking at evidence that would support the teacher in improving the lesson;

- **Conclusion:**
    - *General:* The teacher draws conclusions in a general sense based on the experience and their analysis of their work;
    - *Specific:* The teacher looks at what can be concluded about their own specific and personal situation or way of working;
- **Action plan:** The teacher puts a plan in place to show what they will do differently to improve their teaching based on the conclusions they have reached.

Figure 11.2: Gibbs' Reflection Cycle

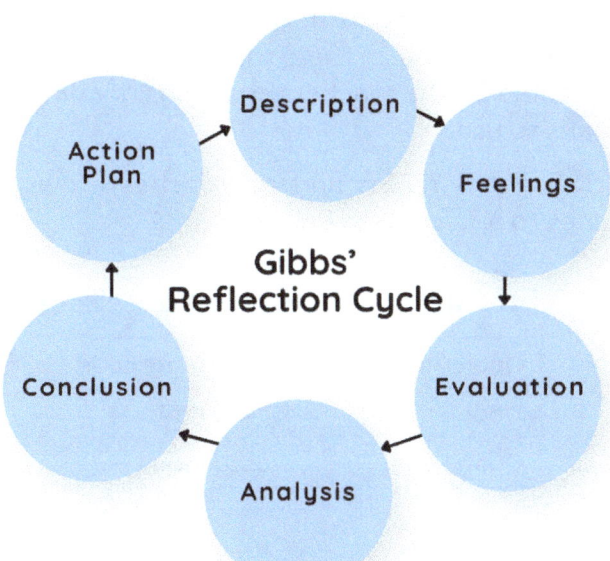

Luttenberg & Bergen (2008) emphasise that reflection must also be both broad and deep. 'Broad reflection' is focused on the content, whereas 'deep reflection' is focused on the nature of the reflection (see below for further elaboration). To enable meaningful reflection, they suggest that reflection entails three domains and two approaches.

The three domains of broad reflection include:

- **Pragmatic:** Focuses on situations in terms of objectives and means; the teacher reflects on a situation with a clear objective in mind. Interestingly, a conclusion reached by pragmatic reflection and the subsequent actions may not be naturally linked because a teacher may know the right action to take but may choose a different action for pragmatic reasons;

- **Ethical:** Relates to interpreting a situation in terms of what is good. Factors to consider here are the teacher's own self-understanding, identity, manner of living and the extent to which their actions are congruent with the values that they want to instil in others. Unlike pragmatic reflection, ethical reflection requires the teacher to accept the findings from this type of reflection. For example, if the teacher expects certain behaviour from their pupils, they should then demonstrate the same behaviour;

- **Moral:** Looks at a situation in terms of what is just. The teacher considers how people should behave towards each other, the rights and obligations people have towards each other and how to agree to resolve conflicts. Unlike pragmatic or ethical reflection, moral reflection approaches matters from the perspective of the shared interest (rather than that of the individual).

To deepen reflection, the teacher may take a closed or an open approach:
- A **closed approach** is one where there is an accepted idea or body of evidence as to the best approach to deal with the situation. Similarly, there is an accepted idea of what approach does not work;
- An **open approach** to reflection is one where there is uncertainty as to what the correct response is. There may be a range of differing responses possible, so the teacher must consider which one is the most suitable means to use.

Combining the different domains and approaches allows a typology of six different approaches to reflection to emerge:

Table 11.6: Luttenberg & Bergen's Six Reflection Types

Open Pragmatic	Closed Pragmatic
Open Ethical	Closed Ethical
Open Moral	Closed Moral

Closed approaches are more common than open approaches, and the pragmatic and ethical domains are more commonly employed by teachers than the moral domain. Luttenberg & Bergen's typology avoids oversimplifying the reflection process. We view their approach as especially relevant when teaching GCE as it encourages the teacher to move beyond pragmatic considerations to include the ethical and moral domains – both areas are especially relevant in GCE! Moreover, this typology does not involve a hierarchy and each of its elements are interlinked. The teacher must thus consider the implications of the reflection from each domain. To guide this reflection, Luttenberg & Bergen (2008, p.562) suggest responding to the following questions simultaneously:
- In what sense is the conclusion suitable?
- In what sense is the conclusion good?
- In what sense is the conclusion just?

In deepening the reflection process then, questions relating to the teacher's experiential knowledge, the help of others involved and reviewing different theoretical approaches are all essential.

To guide your reflection, we suggest that the reflective cycle as outlined by Gibbs provides a good structure. We propose combining Gibbs' cycle of reflection with the typology suggested by Luttenberg & Bergen in order to more broadly and deeply reflect on your practice in GCE. This reflection will necessarily incorporate the *pragmatic*, *ethical* and *moral* domains of reflection and these will be deepened, where appropriate, by *open and closed reflection*.

It is worth noting again that reflection is an on-going process. It occurs throughout all stages in teaching – planning, instruction and post-instruction. While the formal reflection process occurs after teaching lessons, we suggest that you bear the pragmatic, ethical and moral considerations in mind *throughout* the teaching process.

It is our view that the greatest development that you will make in your journey as a GCE teacher will come through reflecting on your own practice! We have outlined a wide variety of areas to reflect upon, coupled with methods of reflection that will enhance your teaching. We also recommend you revisit the reflective questions and suggestions outlined in **Tables 1.1**, **6.1** and **9.1**. Finally, we suggest that you consider the questions below as part of your reflective practice and use them to guide the pedagogical actions you take.

Table 11.7: Teacher's Self-reflections on the Positive Impact of GCE & Their Pedagogical Actions

Teachers' self-reflections on the positive impact of GCE	Teachers' pedagogical actions
<ul><li>What do you know about GCE? How do you inform yourself? How does that impact your thinking?</li><li>What does GCE mean to you? Why do you see it as important? What elements of your own personal and professional identity impact how you teach it?</li><li>Are you enthusiastic about GCE? Why/Why not? How do you overcome challenges to teaching GCE?</li><li>Do you challenge spurious arguments with evidence? Do you discuss GCE issues with others?</li><li>How do/could you demonstrate the value of GCE to your students?</li><li>How do your values align with GCE?</li><li>Are your attitudes challenged by engaging in GCE?</li></ul>	<ul><li>What do you want your students to know?</li><li>What is your understanding of praxis?</li><li>What praxis methods do you use in the classroom and why?</li><li>How do you use these methods to encourage students to engage in challenging issues?</li><li>How do you challenge traditional power dynamics in your classroom?</li><li>What does your classroom look like?</li><li>Does the physical arrangement of the space help you to encourage students to discuss ideas and topics with each other?</li><li>How do you encourage reflective moments in the classroom?</li><li>How do/could you assess your students' learning in GCE?</li><li>What skills do you promote?</li><li>Do you teach in the 'tip'?</li><li>Do you share your own perspective?</li></ul>

Conclusion

Becoming and developing as a GCE teacher often requires a reset in your thinking. While there are unquestionable challenges in teaching GCE, we believe that it is important to acknowledge them, understand the need to overcome them and decide how best to do so. It is our contention that, by developing 'global competence', embracing discussion of topical and sometimes 'controversial' issues, becoming aware of how your identity impacts your teaching and how it can be used to develop it, considering the assessment of your students and primarily reflecting on all these elements and implementing changes that you have identified as necessary, you will develop continuously as a GCE teacher. It is our view that the main criteria in becoming a GCE teacher are the capacity to engage with the discipline with an open mind and the will to strive towards to being a good global citizen. We hope you have found this *Handbook* valuable in guiding you in your growth as a GCE practitioner. GCE aims to provide a future that is fair for all and we are delighted that you are making your own journey to make that difference. Thank you and best wishes.

Seánín Hoy, Gearóid O'Brien & Stephen O'Brien

Appendix

Portrait Values Questionnaire (Schwartz, 2003, pp.313-314)

Here we briefly describe some people. Please read each description and think about how much each person is or is not like you. Tick the box to the right that shows how much the person in the description is like you.

	MALE RESPONDENTS	How much is this person like you?					
		Very much like me	Like me	Somewhat like me	A little like me	Not like me	Not like me at all
G1	Thinking up new ideas and being creative is important to him. He likes to do things in his own original way.						
G2	It is important to him to be rich. He wants to have a lot of money and expensive things.						
G3	He thinks it is important that every person in the world should be treated equally. He believes everyone should have equal opportunities in life.						
G4	It's important to him to show his abilities. He wants people to admire what he does.						
G5	It is important to him to live in secure surroundings. He avoids anything that might endanger his safety.						
G6	He likes surprises and is always looking for new things to do. He thinks it is important to do lots of different things in life.						
G7	He believes that people should do what they are told. He thinks people should follow rules at all times, even when no-one is watching.						
G8	It is important to him to listen to people who are different from him. Even when he disagrees with them, he still wants to understand them.						
G9	It is important to him to be humble and modest. He tries not to draw attention to himself.						
G10	Having a good time is important to him. He likes to "spoil" himself.						
G11	It is important to him to make his own decisions about what he does. He likes to be free and not depend on others.						

		How much is this person like you?					
	MALE RESPONDENTS	Very much like me	Like me	Some-what like me	A little like me	Not like me	Not like me at all
G12	It's very important to him to help the people around him. He wants to care for their well-being.						
G13	Being very successful is important to him. He hopes people will recognise his achievements.						
G14	It is important to him that the government ensures his safety against all threats. He wants the state to be strong so it can defend its citizens.						
G15	He looks for adventures and likes to take risks. He wants to have an exciting life.						
G16	It is important to him always to behave properly. He wants to avoid doing anything people would say is wrong.						
G17	It is important to him to get respect from others. He wants people to do what he says.						
G18	It is important to him to be loyal to his friends. He wants to devote himself to people close to him.						
G19	He strongly believes that people should care for nature. Looking after the environment is important to him.						
G20	Tradition is important to him. He tries to follow the customs handed down by his religion or his family.						
G21	He seeks every chance he can to have fun. It is important to him to do things that give him pleasure.						

| | FEMALE RESPONDENTS | \multicolumn{6}{c}{How much is this person like you?} |
		Very much like me	Like me	Some-what like me	A little like me	Not like me	Not like me at all
G1	Thinking up new ideas and being creative is important to her. She likes to do things in her own original way.						
G2	It is important to her to be rich. She wants to have a lot of money and expensive things.						
G3	She thinks it is important that every person in the world should be treated equally. She believes everyone should have equal opportunities in life.						
G4	It's important to her to show her abilities. She wants people to admire what she does.						
G5	It is important to her to live in secure surroundings. She avoids anything that might endanger her safety.						
G6	She likes surprises and is always looking for new things to do. She thinks it is important to do lots of different things in life.						
G7	She believes that people should do what they are told. She thinks people should follow rules at all times, even when no-one is watching.						
G8	It is important to her to listen to people who are different from her. Even when she disagrees with them, she still wants to understand them.						
G9	It is important to her to be humble and modest. She tries not to draw attention to herself.						
G10	Having a good time is important to her. She likes to "spoil" herself.						
G11	It is important to her to make her own decisions about what she does. She likes to be free and not depend on others.						
G12	It's very important to her to help the people around her. She wants to care for their well-being.						
G13	Being very successful is important to her. She hopes people will recognise her achievements.						

FEMALE RESPONDENTS		How much is this person like you?					
		Very much like me	Like me	Some-what like me	A little like me	Not like me	Not like me at all
G14	It is important to her that the government ensures her safety against all threats. She wants the state to be strong so it can defend its citizens.						
G15	She looks for adventures and likes to take risks. She wants to have an exciting life.						
G16	It is important to her always to behave properly. She wants to avoid doing anything people would say is wrong.						
G17	It is important to her to get respect from others. She wants people to do what she says.						
G18	It is important to her to be loyal to her friends. She wants to devote herself to people close to her.						
G19	She strongly believes that people should care for nature. Looking after the environment is important to her.						
G20	Tradition is important to her. She tries to follow the customs handed down by her religion or her family.						
G21	She seeks every chance she can to have fun. It is important to her to do things that give her pleasure.						

REFERENCES

Andreotti, V. (2006). 'Soft *versus* critical global citizenship education', *Policy & Practice: A Development Education Review*, 3(Autumn), pp.40-51.

Andreotti, V., Stein, S., Sutherland, A., Pashby, K., Susa, R. & Amsler, S. (2018) 'Mobilising different conversations about global justice in education: Toward alternative futures in uncertain times', *Policy & Practice: A Development Education Review*, 26(Spring), pp.9-41.

Arendt, H. (1968). *Between Past & Future: Eight Exercises in Political Thought*. New York: The Viking Press.

Banks, J.A. (2008). 'Diversity, group identity, and citizenship education in a global age', *Educational Researcher*, 37(3), pp.129-139, doi: 10.3102/0013189X08317501

Beauchamp, C. & Thomas, L. (2009). 'Understanding teacher identity: an overview of issues in the literature and implications for teacher education', *Cambridge Journal of Education*, 39(2), pp.175–189. doi: 10.1080/03057640902902252.

Bellucci-Buckelew, M. & Fishman, A. (2011). *Reaching & Teaching Diverse Populations: Strategies for Moving beyond Stereotypes*. Thousand Oaks, CA: Sage.

Bilston, B. (2022) *Refugees*. London: Palazzo Editions.

Bouchard, N. (2002). 'A narrative approach to moral experience using dramatic play and writing', *Journal of Moral Education*, 31(4), pp.407-422.

Boulianne, S. & Theocharis, Y. (2020). 'Young people, digital media, and engagement: A meta-analysis of research', *Social Science Computer Review*, 38(2), pp.111-127.

Bourdieu, P. (1986). The Forms of Capital, in Richardson, J.G. (Ed., pp.241-258). *Handbook of Theory & Research for the Sociology of Education*. New York: Greenwood Press.

boyd, D. (2014). It's Complicated: The Social Lives of Networked Teens. New Haven, Connecticut: Yale University Press.

Boyer, B.T., Kahne, J.E. & Middaugh, E. (2015). 'Youth comprehension of political messages in YouTube videos', *New Media & Society*, 19(4), pp.522-541, doi: 10.1177/1461444815611593.

Bryan, A. (2011). 'Professionalism and deradicalisation of development education', *Policy & Practice – A Development Education Review*, 12, pp.1-14.

Bryan, A. (2012). 'You've got to teach people that racism is wrong and then they won't be racist: Curricular representations and young people's understandings of race and racism', *Journal of Curriculum Studies*, 44(5), pp.599-629.

Bryan, A. (2022). 'Pedagogy of the implicated: advancing a social ecology of responsibility framework to promote deeper understanding of the climate crisis'. *Pedagogy, Culture & Society*. 30(3), pp.329-348.

Campbell, M., Callaghan, A., Lehane, L., Mylotte, L., O'Shea, U. & Shanahan, M. (2023). *Embedding Global Citizenship in Pedagogical Practices: Samples from Practice*. Sligo. St. Angela's College Publication.

Chandra, S. (2020). Understanding Refugees through *Home* by Warsan Shire. E International.

Collier, P. (2013). *Exodus: Immigration and Multiculturalism in the 21st Century*. London: Penguin Group.

Common Sense Media (2023). Five questions to ask about media. Available at: https://www.commonsense.org/sites/default/files/pdf/2017-11/5-questions-to-ask-about-media-student-teacher_0.pdf (Accessed: 11 April 2024).

Conway, P., Murphy, R., Hall, K., Kitching, K., Long, F., McKeon, J., Murphy, B., O'Brien, S. & O'Sullivan, D. (2011). *Learning to Teach Study (LETS): Developing Curricular & Cross-curricular Competences in Becoming a 'Good' Secondary Teacher*. Dublin: DES Publications.

Costa, A.L. (2000). 'Describing 16 habits of mind', Habits of Mind: A Developmental Series.

Crisis UK (2019). Crisis | Together we will end homelessness. [online] Available at: https://www.crisis.org.uk/.

CSO (2024). *Population & Migration Estimates*, April 2024. Available at: https://www.cso.ie/en/releasesandpublications/ep/p-pme/populationandmigrationestimatesapril2024/ (Accessed: 01 September 2024).

Daly, T., Regan, C. & Regan, C. (eds., 2016). 80-20: Development in an Unequal World (7th edition). Bray, Ireland: Educating & Acting for a Better World / London: New Internationalist Publications.

Davis, B.G. (2009). *Tools for Teaching* (2nd edition). San Francisco, CA: Jossey-Bass.

Day, L. (2002). '"Putting Yourself in Other People's Shoes": The use of Forum theatre to explore refugee and homeless issues in schools', *Journal of Moral Education*, 31(1), pp.21-34.

Dolan, A. (Ed, 2024). *Teaching the Sustainable Development Goals to Young Citizens (10-16 years): A focus on teaching hope, respect, empathy and advocacy in schools*. London & New York. Routledge.

Donnelly, V., Hoy, S. & O'Brien, S. (2023). 'Student teachers' experiences of doing Development and Global Citizenship Education in the post-primary classroom'. Video production in conjunction with Chroma Films, June 1, 2023. See Make an Impact with Research in Education | University College Cork (ucc.ie).

Druckman, J.N. (2012). 'The politics of motivation', *Critical Review*, 24(2), pp. 199–216, doi: 10.1080/08913811.2012.711022.

Dunn, J. (2016). 'Demystifying process drama: Exploring the why, what, and how', *NJ: Drama Australia Journal*, 40(2), pp.127–140, doi: 10.1080/14452294.2016.1276738.

Elliott, V., Fukazawa, H., Ikeno, N., Shawyer, S.O.C., Watanabe, J. & Davies, I. (2015). 'Drama and citizenship education in England and Japan', *Teaching Citizenship*, 41(Spring), pp.50-51.

Estés, C.P. (2008). *Women Who Run with the Wolves: Contacting the Power of the Wild Woman*. New York: Random House.

European Commission (2024). Statistics on migration to Europe. Available at: https://commission.europa.eu/strategy-and-policy/priorities-2019-2024/promoting-our-european-way-life/statistics-migration-europe_en#employment-of-immigrants (Accessed: 19 May 2024).

Fletcher, L. (2023). Numbers in direct provision double to 20,000 in a year. Available at: https://www.rte.ie/news/ireland/2023/0312/1361762-direct-provision/ (Accessed: 31 May 2024).

Fook, J. (2010). Beyond reflective practice: Reworking the 'critical' in critical reflection. In Bradbury, H., Frost, N., Kilminster, S & Zucas, M. (eds.), *Beyond Reflective Practice: New Approaches to Professional Lifelong Learning* (pp. 37-51). London: Routledge.

Freire, P. (1996). *Pedagogy of the Oppressed*. Original publication in 1968. London: Penguin.

Freire, P. (2014). *Pedagogy of Hope: Reliving Pedagogy of the Oppressed*. Original publication in 1992. London & New York: Bloomsbury.

Gibbs, G. (1988). *Learning by Doing: A Guide to Teaching & Learning Methods*. Oxford: Further Education Unit.

Giroux, H. (2020). *On Critical Pedagogy* (2nd edition). London: Bloomsbury.

Gleason, B. & Von Gillern, S. (2018). 'Digital citizenship with social media: Participatory practices of teaching and learning in secondary education', *Journal of Educational Technology & Society*, 21(1), pp.200-212.

Golden, B. (Ed, 2024). *Global Citizenship Education – Curious Teachers Critical Classrooms*. Maynooth. DICE (Development & Intercultural Education) publication.

Goren, H. & Yemini, M. (2017). 'The global citizenship education gap: Teacher perceptions of the relationship between global citizenship education and students' socio-economic status', *Teaching & Teacher Education*, 67, pp.9-22.

Government of Ireland (2022). *ESD to 2030: Second National Strategy on Education for Sustainable Development*. Dublin: Government Publications.

Greene, J.P., Erickson, H.H., Watson, A.R. & Beck, M.I. (2018). 'The "Play's the Thing": Experimentally examining the social and cognitive effects of school field trips to live theater performances', *Educational Researcher*, 47(4), pp.246-254, doi: 10.3102/0013189X18761034.

Gundara, J. (2008). 'Civilisational knowledge, interculturalism and citizenship education', *Intercultural Education*, 19(6), pp.469–479, doi: 10.1080/14675980802568269.

Gundara, J.S. (2010). Citizenship and intercultural education in an international and comparative context. In Grant, C. & Portera, A. (eds.), *Intercultural & Multicultural Education: Enhancing Global Interconnectedness* (pp.294-314). New York, NY: Routledge.

Guo, L. (2014). 'Preparing teachers to educate for 21st century global citizenship: Envisioning and enacting', *Journal of Global Citizenship & Equity Education*, 4(1), pp.1-23.

Hagan, M. & McGlynn, C. (2004). 'Moving barriers: Promoting learning for diversity in Initial Teacher Education,' *Intercultural Education*, 15, pp.243-252.

Hanel, P.H.P., Foad, C. & Maio, G.R. (2021). Attitudes & Values. In: *Oxford Research Encyclopedia of Psychology*. Oxford: Oxford University Press (OUP).

Hargittai, E., Fullerton, L., Menchen-Trevino, E. & Thomas, K.Y. (2010). 'Trust online: Young adults' evaluation of web content', *International Journal of Communication*, 4(1), pp.468–494.

Hayden, S. (2022). *My Fourth Time, We Drowned: Seeking Refuge on the World's Deadliest Migration Route*. London: 4th Estate.

Hess, D.E. (2009). *Controversy in the Classroom: The Democratic Power of Discussion*. New York: Routledge.

Hess, D.E. & McAvoy, P. (2014). *The Political Classroom: Evidence & Ethics in Democratic Education*. London and New York: Routledge.

Hobbs, R. (2017). *Create to Learn: Introduction to Digital Literacy*. Malden, MA: John Wiley & Sons.

Hobbs, R. (2020). *Mind over Media: Propaganda Education for a Digital Age*. New York: WW Norton & Company.

Hobbs, R. (2021). *Media Literacy in Action: Questioning the Media*. London: Rowman & Littlefield Publishers.

Homelessness in Ireland (n.d.). Homepage. Available at: https://homelessnessinireland.ie/ (Accessed: 31 May 2024).

hooks, b. (2010). Teaching Critical Thinking: Practical Wisdom. New York: Routledge.

Horton, M. & Freire, P. (1990). *We Make the Road by Walking: Conversations on Education & Social Change*. Edited by B. Bell, J. Gaventa & J. Peters. Philadelphia, PA: Temple University Press.

Hoy, S. (2024). The critical state of Global Citizenship Education (GCE) in Initial Teacher Education (ITE) in Ireland: An exploration of student teachers' experiences of a 'praxis' curriculum design to promote greater inclusion, equality and active participation in global democratic societies. University College Cork. Unpublished PhD Thesis.

Hoy, S. & O'Brien, S. (2022). *Introducing Development and Global Citizenship Education: A Guide for Teachers*. Video production in conjunction with Chroma Films, Dec 1, 2022. See Make an Impact with Research in Education | University College Cork (ucc.ie)

Huo, Y., Cheng, H. & Xie, J. (2023). 'Laying the foundations of phronesis (practical wisdom) through moral dilemma discussions in Chinese primary schools', *Journal of Moral Education*, pp.1–18, doi: 10.1080/03057240.2023.2291990.

IDEA (2021). *Irish Aid Development Education Strategy 2017-2023*. Available at: https://www.irishaid.ie/media/irishaid/allwebsitemedia/20newsandpublications/publicationpdfsenglish/Development-Education-Strategy-2017-2023.pdf (Accessed: 20 June 2021).

Irish Aid (2017). *Irish Aid Development Education Strategy 2017-2023: Strengthening Ireland's Contribution to a Sustainable and Just World through Development Education*. Dublin. Department of Foreign Affairs & Trade.

John, P. & Morris, Z. (2004). 'What are the origins of social capital? Results from a panel survey of young people', *British Elections & Parties Review*, 14(1), pp.94-112, doi: 10.1080/1368988042000258790.

Kahne, J. & Bowyer, B. (2017). 'Educating for democracy in a partisan age: Confronting the challenges of motivated reasoning and misinformation', *American Educational Research Journal*, 54(1), pp.3-34, doi: 10.3102/0002831216679817.

Kahne, J., Lee, N.J. & Feezell, J.T. (2012). 'Digital media literacy education and online civic and political participation', *International Journal of Communication*, 6, pp.1–24, doi: 1932–8036/201200050001.

Kim, Y. (2021). 'Imagining and teaching citizenship as non-citizens: Migrant social studies teachers' positionalities and citizenship education in turbulent times', *Theory & Research in Social Education*, 49(2), pp.176–200. https://doi.org/10.1080/00933104.2021.1885543.

King, A. (1994). Guiding knowledge construction in the classroom: Effects of teaching children how to question and how to explain, *American Educational Research Journal*, 31(2), pp.338-368.

Kvalnes, Ø. (2019). Moral Reasoning at Work: Rethinking Ethics in Organisations. Berlin: Springer Nature. Available at: https://link.springer.com/book/10.1007/978-3-030-15191-1?utm_source=getftr&utm_medium=getftr&utm_campaign=getftr_pilot (Accessed: 27 April 2024).

Ladson-Billings, G. (1995). 'Toward a theory of culturally relevant pedagogy'. *American Educational Research Journal*. 32(3), pp.465-491.

Ladson-Billings, G. (2009). Race still matters: Critical Race Theory in education. In Apple, M.W. Au, W. & Gandin, L.A. (eds.), *The Routledge International Handbook of Critical Education* (pp.110-122). London and New York: Routledge.

Leonardo, Z. (2009). *Race, whiteness and education*. London and New York: Routledge.

Luttenberg, J. & Bergen, T. (2008). 'Teacher reflection: The development of a typology', *Teachers & Teaching*, 14(5-6), pp.543-566.

Madison, N. & Klang, M. (2020). 'The case for digital activism: Refuting the fallacies of slacktivism.' *Journal of Digital Social Research*, 2(2), pp.28-47.

Marchi, R. (2012). 'With Facebook, blogs, and fake news, teens reject journalistic "objectivity"', *Journal of Communication Inquiry*, 36(3), pp.246-262.

Martens, H. & Hobbs, R. (2015). 'How media literacy supports civic engagement in a digital age', *Atlantic Journal of Communication*, 23(2), pp.120-137, doi: 10.1080/15456870.2014.961636.

McCarthy, B. (2022). Viral videos keep clipping President Biden's words out of context. Available at: https://www.poynter.org/reporting-editing/2022/viral-videos-keep-clipping-president-bidens-words-out-of-context/ (Accessed: 10 April 2024).

McGuirk, N. (2023). *Anti-racism Education in Educate Together Primary Schools: An Exploration of Teachers' Conceptualisations and Practices*. Dublin City University. Doctoral dissertation,

Mihailidis, P. & Viotty, S. (2017). 'Spreadable spectacle in digital culture: Civic expression, fake news, and the role of media literacies in "post-fact" society', *American Behavioral Scientist*, 61(4), pp.441-454.

Mikkelson, D. (2011). Did Sarah Palin say: 'I Can See Russia from My House'? Available at https://www.snopes.com/fact-check/sarah-palin-russia-house/ (Accessed: 10 April 2024).

Misco, T. (2018). Morality. In Davies, I., Ho, L., Kiwan, D., Peck, C.L., Peterson, A., Sant, E. & Waghid, Y. (eds.), *The Palgrave Handbook of Global Citizenship & Education* (pp.363-376). London: Palgrave Macmillan.

Neelands, J. & Goode, T. (2015). *Structuring Drama Work* (3rd edition). Cambridge: Cambridge University Press.

Noddings, N. (2003). *Happiness & Education*. New York: Cambridge University Press.

O'Brien, C. & Cassidy, C. (2014). *The Outsiders: Our Teenage Life Behind Barriers*. RTÉ documentary.

O'Brien, G. (2021). 'Flipped learning as a tool to enhance digital citizenship: How teachers' experiences of online teaching during the Covid-19 pandemic can encourage participatory and justice-oriented citizenship', *Citizenship Teaching & Learning*, 16(2), pp.213-223.

O'Brien, G. (2023a). 'History repeating itself: An investigation of the challenges of teaching civic, social and political education', *Irish Educational Studies*, pp.1–22, doi: 10.1080/03323315.2023.2189134.

O'Brien, G. (2023b). 'Differences in the teaching of civic, social and political education: An analysis of the impact of school gender', *Education, Citizenship & Social Justice*, 18(2), pp.161-18, doi: 10.1177/17461979211062118.

O'Brien, G. (2023c). 'Teachers' perceptions of cultural capital: How do they influence the teaching of civic, social and political education?' *Journal of Social Science Education*, 22(4), doi: 10.11576/jsse-6321.

O'Brien, G. (2023d). 'Teacher gender in citizenship education: Does it make a difference?' *Citizenship, Social & Economics Education*, 22(1), pp.3-17.

O'Brien, S. (2016). *Inside Education. Exploring the Art of Good Learning*. London and New York: Routledge.

O'Brien, S. (2024). On navigating 'disruptive' change: The 'anchoring' power of Global Citizenship Education (GCE) for adult educators. In Jõgi, L., Zarifis, G., Gravani, M. & Lattke, S. (eds.), *Adult Educators in the Face of Crisis in Europe: Managing Challenges, Shaping Identities & Changing Cultures*. Leiden: Brill.

O'Brien, S. & Cotter, G. (2018). 'Critical researchers of and for our times': Exploring student teachers' use of critical multicultural and development education frameworks in their professional research papers', *Policy & Practice – A Development Education Review*, 26, pp.74-104.

Ofcom (2019). Children and parents: Media use and attitudes report 2018. Available at https://www.ofcom.org.uk/__data/assets/pdf_file/0024/134907/children-and-parents-media-use-and-attitudes-2018.pdf (Accessed: 31 May 2024).

Olusanya, F. (2021). *Deconstructed*, 22 November, online: https://youtu.be/h9GLR6XNNog . (Accessed: 10 June 2024).

Oxfam (2015). Global Citizenship in the Classroom: A Guide for Teachers. Available at: https://oxfamilibrary.openrepository.com/bitstream/handle/10546/620105/edu-global-citizenship-teacher-guide-091115-en.pdf?sequence=9&isAllowed=y (Accessed: 24 October 2023).

Pashby, K. (2018). 'Identity, belonging and diversity in education for global citizenship: Multiplying, intersecting, transforming, and engaging lived realities'. In Davies, I., Ho, L., Kiwan, D., Peck, C.L., Peterson, A., Sant, E. & Waghid, Y. (eds.), *The Palgrave Handbook of Global Citizenship & Education* (pp.277-293). London: Palgrave Macmillan.

PDST (2011). *Spotlight on Stereotyping: A Resource for Teachers of Civic, Social and Political Education*. Dublin: The Equality Authority.

Pennington, M.C. & Richards, J.C. (2016). 'Teacher identity in language teaching: Integrating personal, contextual, and professional factors', *RELC Journal*, 47(1), pp.5-23.

Pew Research Center (2022). Majority of teens use YouTube, TikTok, Instagram, Snapchat; share of teens who use Facebook dropped sharply from 2014-15 to now. Available at: https://www.pewresearch.org/internet/2022/08/10/teens-social-media-and-technology-2022/pj_2022-08-10_teens-and-tech_0-08/ (Accessed: 10 April 2024).

Pipher, M. (2007). *Writing to Change the World: An Inspiring Guide for Transforming the World with Words*. New York: Penguin.

Pomerantsev, P. (2019). *This Is Not Propaganda: Adventures in the War against Reality*. London: Faber & Faber.

Prowse, A. & Forsyth, R. (2018). Global Citizenship Education: Assessing the Unassessable? In Davies, I., Ho, L., Kiwan, D., Peck, C.L., Peterson, A., Sant, E. & Waghid, Y. (eds.), *The Palgrave Handbook of Global Citizenship & Education*. London: Palgrave Macmillan, pp.607-623.

Quaynor, L. & Murillo, A. (2018). Migration and Implications for Global Citizenship Education: Tensions and Perspectives. In Davies, I., Ho, L., Kiwan, D., Peck, C.L., Peterson, A., Sant, E. and Waghid, Y. (eds.), *The Palgrave Handbook of Global Citizenship & Education*. London: Palgrave Macmillan, pp.425-438.

Rosenshine, B. (2012). 'Principles of instruction: Research-based strategies that all teachers should know', *American Educator*, 36(1), pp.12-19.

Rosling, H., Rosling, O. & Rosling Rönnlund, A. (2018). *Factfulness: Ten Reasons We're Wrong about the World – and Why Things Are Better than You Think*. London: Sceptre.

Rothberg, M. (2019). *The Implicated Subject: Beyond Victims & Perpetrators*. Stanford, CA. Stanford University Press.

Ruiz, P.O. & Vallejos, R.M. (1999). 'The role of compassion in moral education', *Journal of Moral Education*, 28(1), pp.5–17, doi: 10.1080/030572499103278.

Rutter, J. (2012). Migration. In Cowan, P. & Maitles, H. (eds.). *Teaching Controversial Issues in the Classroom: Key Issues & Debates*, (pp.211-223). London: Continuum International.

Saddington, L. & McConnell, F. (2024). 'Simulating alternative internationals: Geopolitics role-playing in UK schools', *Geoforum*, 151.

Sansone, D. (2017). 'Why does teacher gender matter?', *Economics of Education Review*, 61, pp.9-18.

Saturday Night Live (2017). *Thank You, Scott* – SNL. Available at: https://www.youtube.com/watch?v=QDydKwmrHFo (Accessed: 08 April 2024).

Sayed, D. (2022). *Escape from War to Live in Peace*. Waterford: Waterford City & County Council.

Schkade, D., Sunstein, C.R. & Hastie, R. (2007). 'What happened on deliberation day?', *California Law Review*, 95(3), pp.915-940, doi: 10.2139/ssrn.911646.

Schuitema, J., Dam, G.T. & Veugelers, W. (2008). 'Teaching strategies for moral education: A review', *Journal of Curriculum Studies*, 40(1), pp.69-89.

Schwartz, S. H. (2003). A proposal for measuring value orientations across nations. Chapter 7 in the *Questionnaire Development Report of the European Social Survey*, pp.259-319.

Schwartz, S.H. (2012). 'An overview of the Schwartz theory of basic values'. *Online Readings in Psychology & Culture*, 2(1), pp. 1-20.

Shire, W. (2021). 'Conversations about Home', *Transition*, 132, pp.341-481.

Shor, I. (1992). *Empowering Education: Critical Teaching for Social Change*. Chicago: University of Chicago Press.

Simpson, J. (2019). 'Learning to unlearn': Moving educators from a charity mentality towards a social justice mentality. In P. Bamber (ed.). *Teacher Education for Sustainable Development & Global Citizenship*, (pp.40-52). London and New York. Routledge.

Sinatra, G.M. & Lombardi, D. (2020). 'Evaluating sources of scientific evidence and claims in the post-truth era may require reappraising plausibility judgments', *Educational Psychologist*, 55(3), pp.120-131.

sites.lsa.umich.edu. (*n.d.*). Personal Identity Wheel – Inclusive Teaching. [online] Available at: https://sites.lsa.umich.edu/inclusive-teaching/personal-identity-wheel/ (Accessed: 31 May 2024).

Sundar, S.S. (2008). *The MAIN Model: A Heuristic Approach to Understanding Technology Effects on Credibility* (pp. 73-100). Cambridge, MA: MacArthur Foundation Digital Media and Learning Initiative.

Swart, J. & Broersma, M. (2022). 'The trust gap: Young people's tactics for assessing the reliability of political news', *The International Journal of Press/Politics*, 27(2), pp.396-416.

Teaching Council (2020). *Céim: Standards for Initial Teacher Education*. Dublin: Teaching Council Publications.

TIES (Teaching Immigration in European Schools) (*n.d.*). *Migration: A Bird's Eye View*. Available at: https://teachingmigration.eu/module/migration-trends-a-birds-eye-view/ (Accessed: 23 May 2024).

Torchin, L. (2016). What can the Mass Check-in' at Standing Rock Tell Us about Online Advocacy? Available at: https://theconversation.com/what-can-the-mass-check-in-at-standing-rock-tell-us-about-online-advocacy-68276 (Accessed: 20 April 2024).

Tormey, R. & Gleeson, J. (2012). 'The gendering of global citizenship: Findings from a large-scale quantitative study on global citizenship education experiences', *Gender & Education*, 24(6), pp.627–645, doi: 10.1080/09540253.2011.646960.

Tynan, M. (2016). *The Outsiders: Children living in direct provision in Ireland Global Learning Project: Teaching and Learning Unit*. A unit to support Junior Cycle English, using 'The Outsiders: Our teenage life behind barriers,': CDETB Curriculum Development Unit. Available at https://www.worldwiseschools.ie/wp-content/uploads/2018/03/APA_Outsiders_web.pdf?x73158.

UNESCO (2014). *Global Citizenship Education: Preparing Learners for the Challenges of the 21st Century*. Paris: UNESCO.

UNESCO (2015). *Global Citizenship Education: Topics and Learning Objectives*. Available at: https://unesdoc.unesco.org/ark:/48223/pf0000232993 (Accessed: 05 May 2024).

UNHCR (2021). *Teaching about Refugees: Ages 12-15 School Activity Guide*. Available at: https://www.unhcr.org/sites/default/files/legacy-pdf/59d3783d7.pdf (Accessed: 24 May 2024).

UNHCR (*n.d.*) *Emergency Handbook*. Available at: https://emergency.unhcr.org/protection/legal-framework/migrant-definition (Accessed: 17 May 2024).

United Nations (1948). *Universal Declaration of Human Rights*. [online] Available at: https://www.un.org/en/about-us/universal-declaration-of-human-rights. (Accessed: 31 May 2024).

Van Houtum, H.J. & Bueno Lacy, R., (2017). 'The political extreme as the new normal: The cases of Brexit, the French state of emergency and Dutch Islamophobia,' *Fennia*, 195(1), p.85, doi: 10.11143/fennia.64568.

Verducci, S. (2000). 'A moral method? Thoughts on cultivating empathy through method acting', *Journal of Moral Education*, 29(1), pp.87–99, doi: 10.1080/030572400102952.

Veugelers, W. (1997). 'Teaching and learning on moral dilemmas', *American Educational Research Association Conference*, 24-28 March. Chicago.

Vraga, E.K. & Bode, L., (2017). 'Leveraging institutions, educators, and networks to correct misinformation: A commentary on Lewandosky, Ecker & Cook', *Journal of Applied Research in Memory & Cognition*, 6(4), pp.382–388, doi: 10.1016/j.jarmac.2017.09.008.

Waddell, T.F. & Sundar, S.S. (2017). '# thisshowsucks! The overpowering influence of negative social media comments on television viewers', *Journal of Broadcasting & Electronic Media*, 61(2), pp.393-409.

Wells, T. & Sandretto, S. (2017). '"I'm on a journey I never thought I'd be on": Using process drama pedagogy for the literacy programme', *Pedagogies: An International Journal*, 12(2), pp.180–195, doi: 10.1080/1554480X.2016.1245147.

Westheimer, J. & Kahne, J. (2004). 'What kind of citizen? The politics of educating for democracy', *American Educational Research Journal*, 41(2), pp.237-269. https://doi.org/10.3102/00028312041002237.

Whiteley, P. (2014). 'Does citizenship education work? Evidence from a decade of citizenship education in secondary schools in England', *Parliamentary Affairs*, 67: 513–535, doi: 10.1093/pa/gss083.

Wood, B.E. (2014). 'Participatory capital: Bourdieu and citizenship education in diverse school communities', *British Journal of Sociology of Education*, 35(4), pp.578-597, doi: 10.1080/01425692.2013.777209

Zimmer, C. (2004). 'Whose life would you save?', *Discover*, 25(4), pp.60-65.

Zimmerman, J. & Robertson, E. (2017). *The Case for Contention: Teaching Controversial Issues in American Schools*. Chicago: University of Chicago Press.

ABOUT THE AUTHORS

Seánín Hoy is a Ph.D. candidate in UCC, specialising in student teachers' experiences of engaging with GCE and a praxis curriculum design in the post-primary setting. She has co-published video publications on developing understandings of GCE and student teachers' initial experiences engaging with GCE and a praxis pedagogical approach. She is also a practising post-primary teacher.

Gearóid O'Brien lectures on the Professional Master of Education (PME) programme in University College Cork in the Teaching of Civic, Social & Political Education (CSPE). He has published articles on citizenship education, digital citizenship and media literacy and is the author of the CSPE textbook *Call to Action*. He is also a practising post-primary teacher and an advisor to the Teaching Council on Politics & Society.

Dr. Stephen O'Brien (https://publish.ucc.ie./researchprofiles/A013/sobrien) is a senior lecturer in the School of Education, University College Cork. He has taught and published widely in the areas of educational inclusion, multicultural education, and adult education and has served as Principal and Co-Investigator on a number of national and international research projects. He actively designs and manages new curricular and research opportunities for student and practising teachers in the discipline of Global Citizenship Education.